THE
FEAR
OF THE
LORD

*Discover the Key to
Intimately Knowing God*

THE
FEAR

OF THE
LORD

*Discover the Key to
Intimately Knowing God*

JOHN BEVERE

CREATION
HOUSE
Orlando, FL

THE FEAR OF THE LORD by John Bevere
Published by Creation House
Strang Communications Company
600 Rinehart Road, Lake Mary, Florida 32746
Web site: http://www.creationhouse.com

Unless otherwise noted, all Scripture quotations are from the
New King James Version of the Bible. Copyright © 1979, 1980, 1982
by Thomas Nelson, Inc., publishers. Used by permission.

Scripture quotations marked NIV are from the Holy Bible,
New International Version. Copyright © 1973, 1978, 1984,
International Bible Society. Used by permission.

Scripture quotations marked NLT are from the Holy Bible,
New Living Translation, copyright © 1996.
Used by permission of Tyndale House Publishers, Inc.,
Wheaton, IL 60189. All rights reserved.

Scripture quotations marked AMP are from the Amplified Bible.
Old Testament copyright © 1965, 1987 by the Zondervan Corporation.
The Amplified New Testament copyright © 1954, 1958, 1987
by the Lockman Foundation. Used by permission.

Scripture quotations marked KJV are from the
King James Version of the Bible.

Library of Congress Cataloging-in-Publication Data:
Bevere, John.
The fear of the Lord : discover the key to intimately knowing God / John
Bevere.
         p.   cm.
    ISBN: 0-88419-486-8 (pbk.)
    1. God—Worship and live. 2. God—Knowableness. 3. Fear of God
4. Judgment of God. I. Title
BV4817.B48 1997
231'.042—dc21   97-35841
                                            CIP

Printed in the United States of America

8901234 BBG 87654

I would like to dedicate
this book to my wife, Lisa.
I am a privileged man to be married
to such a woman. It would take another book to tell
of her virtues and godly character, but to sum
up her life in one statement, it would be:
She is a woman who fears the Lord.

"She opens her mouth with wisdom, and on her tongue is
the law of kindness.
She watches over the ways of her household, and does not
eat the bread of idleness.
Her children rise up and call her blessed; her husband also,
and he praises her:
'Many daughters have done well, but you excel them all.'
Charm is deceitful and beauty is passing, but a woman
who fears the Lord, she shall be praised."

—PROVERBS 31:26–30

I am grateful to You,
Father, for Your daughter, Lisa Bevere.

My deepest appreciation to . . .

My wife, Lisa. Next to the Lord, you are my greatest love and treasure. Thank you for the hours of editing you contributed to this book. I love you, sweetheart!

Our four sons. All of you have brought great joy to my life. Thank you for sharing in the call of God and encouraging me to travel and to write.

My parents, John and Kay Bevere. Thank you for initially teaching me the fear of the Lord through the godly lifestyle you exemplified.

Those who have taken the time and given a portion of their lives to teach and show me the ways of the kingdom I have seen different facets of Jesus in each of you.

The staff of John Bevere Ministries. Thank you for your unwavering support and faithfulness. Lisa and I love each of you dearly.

The entire Creation House staff who have labored with us and been so supportive of our ministry. You are a joy to work with.

Most important, my sincere gratitude to my Lord. How can words adequately acknowledge all You have done for me and for Your people? I love You more than I will ever be able to express. I love You forever!

Contents

HOLY FEAR IS THE KEY
TO GOD'S SURE FOUNDATION,
UNLOCKING THE TREASURIES OF
SALVATION, WISDOM, AND
KNOWLEDGE.

INTRODUCTION

IN THE SUMMER of 1994 I was invited to minister at a church in the southern part of the United States. It would end up being one of the most unpleasant ministry experiences I would ever have. Yet out of it, a passionate quest was birthed in my heart to know and understand the fear of the Lord.

Two years prior, this was a church that had experienced a powerful move of God. An evangelist came for a period of four weeks, and the Lord revived this church with His presence. They were experiencing an abundance of what many call "holy laughter." It was so refreshing that the pastor and many of his people did what so often happens; they remained camped at the place of refreshment instead of continuing on to pursue God. They soon developed more interest in manifestations of refreshing than to know the Lord who refreshes.

The second night of our meetings, the Spirit of God led me to preach on the fear of the Lord. At the time my understanding of the fear of the Lord was still forming, but God led me to preach on what He had already shown me from the Scriptures.

The next night I came into the service totally unprepared for what was about to happen. Without any previous discussion, the pastor stood up after praise and worship and spent a considerable amount of time correcting what I had preached the night before. I sat in the front row, almost in shock. The basis of his correction was that New Testament believers do not have to fear God. He backed this up with 1 John 4:18: "There is no fear in love; but perfect love casts out fear, because fear involves torment. But he who fears has not been made perfect in love." He had confused a *spirit of fear* with the *fear of the Lord*.

The following morning I found a deserted area outside my hotel where I spent a considerable amount of time praying. I came before the Lord with an open heart and submitted to any correction He desired to bring to me. I have learned that God's correction is always for my good. He corrects us, that we might be partakers of His holiness (Heb. 12:7–11). Almost immediately I sensed God's overwhelming love. I did not perceive His disappointment with what I had preached, but rather His pleasure. Tears ran down my face in His wonderful presence.

I continued in prayer and, after awhile, found myself crying out from deep within my spirit for the knowledge of the fear of the Lord. I raised my voice, drawing together all my strength from within, and cried, "Father, I want to know and walk in the fear of the Lord!"

When I finished praying I didn't care what I might face in the future. All I wanted was to know His heart. I sensed that my request to learn this facet of His holy nature had deeply pleased Him. Since that day God has been faithful to reveal to me the importance of the fear of the Lord. He has revealed His desire for all believers to know the importance of it as well.

Although I always had known that the fear of the Lord was important, I did not comprehend just how integral it was until God opened my eyes in response to that prayer. I had always seen the *love* of God as the foundation for relationship with the

Lord. I quickly discovered that the fear of the Lord was just as foundational. Isaiah says:

> The Lord is exalted, for he dwells on high; he will fill Zion with justice and righteousness. He will be the sure foundation for your times, a rich store of salvation and wisdom and knowledge; the fear of the Lord is the key to this treasure.
>
> —ISAIAH 33:5–6, NIV

Holy fear is the key to God's sure foundation, unlocking the treasuries of salvation, wisdom, and knowledge. Along with the love of God, it composes the very foundation of life! We will soon learn that we cannot truly love God until we fear Him; nor can we properly fear Him until we love Him.

As I wrote this book, our family was building a new home. I visited the job site many times, and God used these moments to teach me lessons from some of the basic principles of construction. Actual construction begins with the foundation and framing of the house. This will uphold all the finishing components such as the tile, carpet, windows, cabinetry, and paint. Once the house is completed, you no longer see any part of the foundation and framework, although they hold and protect all the beautiful furnishings and finishes inside. Without this framework, you would have little more than a pile of materials.

The same is true with the construction of this book. We will clearly delineate between the fear of God and His judgment, then progress on to an intimate knowledge of Him. We will outline the protection such fear provides from judgment, and conclude with its role in our intimacy with God. Each chapter holds truths that are both informative and transforming. The first several chapters will provide the framework for the rest of the book. It will develop in our spirits the strength to hold what God will reveal.

Read as though this book is a house under construction. Don't jump from the framing to the laying down of carpet. Without a roof, the carpet will need to be replaced before construction is complete. Building is a progression.

Take the time to prayerfully read and understand each chapter before proceeding to the next. Ask the Holy Spirit to reveal God's Word to you through this book, "For the letter kills, but the Spirit gives life" (2 Cor. 3:6).

The fear of the Lord is not grasped by the mind but etched in our hearts. It is revealed by the Holy Spirit as we read His Word. It is one of the manifestations of the Spirit of God (Isa. 11:1–2). God will impart it to the hearts of those who earnestly seek Him (Jer. 29:11–14; 32:40).

Let's pray before we begin:

Father, in the name of Jesus, I have opened this book because I desire to know and understand the holy fear of the Lord. I realize this is impossible without the help of the Holy Spirit. I ask that You would anoint me with Your Spirit. Open my eyes to see, my ears to hear, and my heart that I might know and understand what You are saying to me.

As I read, let me hear Your voice within the words of this book. Transform me, lifting me from one level of glory to another. Then lift me again with the goal of eventually seeing You face to face. Let my life be so transformed that I will never be the same.

For this, I give You all the praise and glory and honor, both now and forever. Amen.

—JOHN BEVERE
ORLANDO, FLORIDA

DO YOU THINK
THE KING OF KINGS AND
LORD OF LORDS IS GOING
TO COME INTO A PLACE WHERE
HE IS NOT GIVEN DUE HONOR
AND REVERENCE?

One

WIND FROM HEAVEN

By those who come near Me I must be regarded as holy; and before all the people I must be glorified.

—LEVITICUS 10:3

IT WAS JUST ten days into the new year of 1997. In those few days I had already been to Europe and Asia to minister. I was excited as I once again boarded a plane, this time to South America. I had never been to the nation of Brazil and was honored to have been invited to speak at a national conference taking place in three of its major cities. After flying all night I was greeted by some very hungry and expectant leaders at the airport. They had been anticipating these meetings, and their enthusiasm revived me.

The first service was held that very evening in the capital city of Brasilia. After a few short hours of rest, my interpreter and I were picked up at our hotel and taken to the meeting. Cars crowded the parking lot and streets, and I could see that the meeting would be well-attended. As we approached the building, I could hear music as it escaped through a five-foot opening left for ventilation between the top wall and roof. My own excitement and anticipation mounted as I listened to the music of familiar praise choruses being sung in Portuguese—the primary language of Brazil.

Once inside, I was ushered directly to the platform. The auditorium, which held approximately four thousand people, was full. The platform was rocking with high-intensity praise music. The music quality was very good, for the musicians were skilled and flowed well together. The singing was also excellent, the leaders gifted with very good voices. Yet I quickly noted a complete absence of the Lord's presence. As I scanned the crowd and musicians, I thought, *Where is God?* So immediately I questioned, *Lord, where is Your presence?*

As I waited for His reply, I noticed what was happening in the building. Through the bright lights of the platform I could see the people milling about. Many stood with their eyes open looking at something or someone in the building. Many appeared to be bored. Their hands were thrust into their pockets or hung heavy at their sides. Everything about their body postures and countenances gave the appearance of a casual crowd waiting patiently for a show to begin. Some talked to one another, and others roamed the aisles, wandering in and out of the auditorium.

I was grieved. This was not an evangelistic outreach but a believer's conference. I knew there may be some in attendance who were not believers, yet I also knew that the majority of those present in this nonchalant crowd were "Christians."

I waited, hoping the people would enter into a true reverence of the Lord. I thought, *Surely this atmosphere will change.* But it didn't. After twenty or thirty minutes, the music tempo slowed to what we call the "worship songs." Yet what I witnessed was far from true worship. This same casual behavior I had observed when I entered the auditorium had moved forward into the service.

When the song service ended, it seemed as if over an hour had transpired, but it was actually less than forty minutes. Those present were told to sit down. They sat, but the underlying rumble of casual conversation continued. One leader took the microphone to exhort the people, yet the people talked on. The leader read from the Bible and taught. The entire time I heard the dull rumble of many voices speaking and many people moving about in the congregation. I also noticed many paying no attention to the speaker. I could scarcely believe what I was witnessing. In frustration, I turned to my Brazilian interpreter and asked if this behavior was normal for their services.

He shared my disgust. "Sometimes I have to address it and ask the people to please pay attention," he whispered. At this point, I was becoming angry. I had been in other meetings where the people behaved this way, but never to this magnitude. In each of those meetings I had encountered a similar spiritual atmosphere—heaviness, void of God's presence. I knew now that my question—*Lord, where is Your presence?*—had been answered. His presence certainly was not here.

The Spirit of God then spoke to me and said, "I want you to directly confront this."

When I was finally introduced, the murmur had diminished but was still present. I stepped up to the podium and stood there looking at the crowd. I was determined to say nothing until I had their attention. I felt godly indignation burning within my breast. After a minute, everyone fell silent, realizing nothing was happening on the platform.

I did not introduce myself or greet the crowd. Instead I opened with this question, "How would you like it if, while you spoke with someone, they ignored you the entire time or continued to carry on a conversation with the person next to them? Or if their eyes roamed with disinterest and disrespect?"

I paused, then answered my own question: "You wouldn't like it, would you?"

I probed further: "What if every time you rang the doorbell to visit a neighbor's house you were greeted with a careless attitude and monotone sigh, 'Oh, it's *you* again; come on in.'"

I paused, then added, "You wouldn't visit them anymore, would you?"

Then I stated firmly, "Do you think the King of kings and Lord of lords is going to come into a place where He is not given due honor and reverence? Do you think the Master of all creation is going to speak when His Word is not respected enough to be listened to attentively? You're deceived if you do!"

I continued, "Tonight when I walked into this building, I did not sense the presence of God at all. Not in the praise, not in the worship, not in the exhortation, or during the offering. There is a reason: The Lord never comes where He is not reverenced. The president of your nation would be granted great honor on this platform tonight simply out of respect for his office. If I stood here with one of your favorite soccer players, many of you would be on the edges of your seats. You would be eagerly anticipating and listening to every word he spoke. Yet while God's Word was read a moment ago, you barely listened, for you esteemed it lightly."

I proceeded to read what God requires of those who come near Him:

> By those who come near Me I must be regarded as holy;
> and before all the people I must be glorified.
> —LEVITICUS 10:3

For the next hour and a half, I preached the message God had burned in my heart. The words came with boldness and authority, and I did not fear what the people would think nor how they would react.

If they run me out of this nation tomorrow, I don't care, I would rather obey God! I told myself—and I meant it.

You could have heard a pin drop in the silent moments between each of my statements. For that hour and a half there was no further crowd noise. There was no further disrespect. The Spirit of God had arrested the people's attention by His Word. The atmosphere was changing by the minute. I could sense the Word of God pounding through the hardened shells of their hearts.

At the close of my message, I asked every person present to close their eyes. The call for repentance was pointed and brief: "If you have treated what God calls holy as common, if you have

4

lived with an irreverent attitude toward the things of God, and if tonight you have been convicted by the Holy Spirit through His Word, are you ready to repent before the Lord? If so, stand to your feet." Without hesitation, 75 percent of those present rose to their feet.

I bowed my head, praying aloud this simple, sincere prayer: "Lord, confirm Your Word preached tonight to these people."

Immediately the presence of the Lord filled that auditorium. Although I had not led the congregation in a prayer, I heard sobs and cries rising from the crowd. It was as if a wave of God's presence had swept through the building, bringing cleansing and refreshing. It was not possible for all present to come forward to the altar, so I led a prayer of repentance that could be prayed from where they stood. I watched as people wiped away tears. His wonderful presence continued.

After a few minutes God's presence subsided. I encouraged the people not to lose their focus on their Master. "Draw near to God and He will draw near to you" (James 4:8).

A few moments passed and another wave of His presence flooded the building. There were more tears as the crying intensified. His presence was even more far-reaching this time, and more people were touched by the Master. This lasted a few minutes, then again subsided. I exhorted the people not to drift between the waves but to hold fast their heart's focus.

A few minutes later I heard the Spirit of God whisper to my heart, "I am coming again." Immediately I sensed it and said, "He's coming again!"

What I now write will in no way accurately represent what happened next. My words are too limited and God too awesome. Neither will I exaggerate, for that would also be irreverent. I interviewed three other leaders who were present to clarify and confirm what I now record.

No sooner had the word "again" left my lips when the following happened. The only way I know how to describe it is to compare it to standing a hundred or so yards away from the end of a runway as a huge jet takes off right in front you. This describes the roar of the wind that immediately blew through that auditorium. Almost simultaneously the people erupted in fervent and intense prayer, their voices rising and combining into almost a single shout.

When I first heard the rushing wind, I reasoned that a jet had just flown over the building. In no way did I want to attribute something to God if there was a chance that it was not. My mind raced to remember the proximity of the airport. It was nowhere nearby, and two hours had passed with no sounds of planes overhead.

I turned inward to the Spirit, realizing I could sense the presence of God in an awesome way, and that the people had exploded into prayer. This was certainly not in response to an airplane's passing overhead.

If it had been a plane, it would have had to have been flying at the low altitude of no more than one hundred yards over the building in order to sound like that. And even at that, I would not have been able to hear such a mighty rushing noise over the din of three thousand people praying loudly.

The sound I heard was much louder, and clearly overpowered all the voices. With it resolved in my mind that the wind was the wind of the Holy Spirit, I still did not say anything. I did not want to relay inaccurate information or hype the people with overzealous professions of spiritual manifestation. The roar of this wind lasted approximately two minutes. When it subsided, it left in its wake a praying, weeping people. The atmosphere was charged with holy reverence. The Lord's presence was very real and powerful.

The awesome aftermath of His presence continued for fifteen to twenty minutes. Then I turned the platform over to the leader and asked to be taken out of the building immediately. Often I linger and talk with others after a service, but now any casual conversation seemed inappropriate. The leaders asked me to join them for dinner, but I declined. Still shaken by His presence, I responded, "No, I just want to go back to my hotel room."

I was escorted to the car. I rode back to the hotel accompanied by my interpreter and a lady and her husband who were leaders. This woman was a recording artist, and her music was popular in the nation.

She entered the car, crying, "Did you hear the wind?"

I quickly responded, "That was an airplane." (Though I sensed in my heart it was not, I wanted confirmation and was determined not to be the first to say anything.)

"No," she stated and shook her head. "It was the Spirit of the Lord."

Then her husband, a man I found to be very quiet and reserved, firmly asserted, "There was no plane anywhere near the building."

"Really!" I exclaimed.

He continued, "Furthermore, the sound of that wind did not come through the soundboard, there was no reading on the board, or record of any noise." I sat silently, in complete awe.

Later I learned the reason this man was so certain that the wind we heard was not caused by an aircraft. There were security personnel and police *outside* who also reported hearing a mighty sound coming from *inside* the building. Outside, no wind. Just another calm Brazilian evening.

His wife continued as tears streamed down her cheeks. "I saw waves of fire falling on the building and angels everywhere!"

I could hardly believe my ears. I had heard this same description used by a minister two months earlier in meetings in North Carolina. I had preached on the fear of the Lord, and God's presence had fallen mightily on those assembled—more than a hundred little children wept profusely for an hour. A visiting minister told the pastor that she had seen waves of balls of fire falling on the building. This was also confirmed by three choir members.

Now, I just wanted to be alone with the Lord. Once in the privacy of my hotel room, all I could do was worship and pray.

I was scheduled to minister at one more service before departing for Rio De Janeiro. This time when I walked into the auditorium, the atmosphere was totally different. I could sense a restored respect for the Lord. This time the music wasn't merely good but void of God's presence; it was wonderful, anointed, and the presence of the Lord was sweet.

David says, "In fear of You I will worship toward Your holy

temple" (Ps. 5:7). All true worship is anchored in a reverence for His presence, for God says, "You shall . . . reverence My sanctuary: I am the Lord" (Lev. 19:30).

In this second service many received deliverance and healing. Many who had been bound by bitterness and had harbored offenses were set free. Where the Lord is reverenced, His presence manifests—and where His presence manifests, needs are met.

Now we can understand David's urgency:

> Oh, fear the Lord, you His saints! There is no want to those who fear Him.
>
> —PSALM 34:9

This is the message you hold in your hands today—the fear of the Lord. In these pages we will search, with the help of the Holy Spirit, not only the meaning of the fear of the Lord but what it is to walk in the treasures of its truth. We will learn of the judgment which comes when there is a lack of holy fear, as well as of the glorious benefits found within fearing God.

THERE ARE PEOPLE WHO ARE QUICK TO ACKNOWLEDGE JESUS AS SAVIOR, HEALER, AND DELIVERER . . . YET THEY REDUCE HIS GLORY TO THE LEVEL OF CORRUPTIBLE MEN BY THEIR ACTIONS AND HEART ATTITUDES.

Two

CHANGED GLORY

For who in the heavens can be compared to the Lord? Who among the sons of the mighty can be likened to the Lord? God is greatly to be feared in the assembly of the saints, and to be held in reverence by all those around Him.

—PSALM 89:6–7

B EFORE discussing the fear of the Lord, we must capture a glimpse of the greatness and glory of the God we serve. The psalmist first declares the awesome wonders of God, then gives the exhortation to fear Him. His words, related in modern vernacular, would be a bold, declarative question: "Who in the universe can compare to the Lord?" He wants us to meditate on God's unfathomable glory. For how can we duly respect and honor Him if we remain unaware of His greatness, or why He deserves it?

FAMOUS, YET UNKNOWN

IN EXPLANATION, let's imagine one who is famous in the most powerful nation on earth. He's a gifted and knowledgeable man. Everyone in his country knows of his greatness and fame. He is an inventor with the most outstanding and

11

significant scientific contributions and discoveries known to man. He is the most outstanding athlete from this country. In fact, no one can compete with him in any arena in life. In addition to all this, he is the king and a very wise ruler. At every level and every place in the country, he is given tremendous respect and honor. Great parades and glorious receptions are held in his honor.

Now, what would happen if this king were to travel to another country where his position and greatness were unknown? What sort of reception would he receive in a strange country, inferior in every way to his great nation?

Although their greatest men are far below the caliber of this ruler, still this noble king decides to visit as an ordinary man—without his royal robes, entourage of nobility, security force, counselors, and servants. He goes alone. How will he be treated?

To put it simply, he will be treated no differently than any other foreigner. Though this man is far greater than the mightiest of the nation, he will be given little or no respect. He may even be treated with contempt at times, simply because he is a foreigner. His inventions and scientific discoveries have greatly benefited this nation, yet still the people do not know him and therefore do not give him the respect and honor he deserves.

Now hear the account of John regarding Jesus, Immanuel, God manifested in the flesh:

> He was in the world, and the world was made through Him, and the world did not know Him. He came to His own, and His own did not receive Him.
>
> —JOHN 1:10–11

It is very sad that the One who created the universe and the very world we live in did not receive the reception and honor He deserved. Even more tragic, He came to His own, the ones who watched for him and knew His covenant, the ones He had delivered time and again by His power; yet He did not receive honor. Though the people spoke of His coming, attended temple regularly in anticipation of His coming, and prayed for the benefits which would accompany His rule, they did not recognize Him when He came.

His own did not recognize the awesome One they professed to serve faithfully. Not only were the Israelites ignorant of the greatness of God's power, but they were equally ignorant of the greatness of His wisdom. It is therefore little wonder that they could not give Him the fear or reverence He deserved. God explained:

> Inasmuch as these people draw near with their mouths and honor Me with their lips, but have removed their hearts far from Me, and their fear toward Me is taught by the commandment of men. . . .
>
> —ISAIAH 29:13

He said, "Their fear toward Me is taught by the commandment of men." He is saying that the people had reduced the glory of the Lord to the glory of corruptible man. They served God in the image they had created—not by His true image, but by their own standards.

CHANGING THE GLORY OF THE INCORRUPTIBLE GOD

THIS WAS NOT isolated to Jesus' generation, though it had reached its all-time low during the time of Jesus. This same error repeated itself throughout the generations of these people who were entrusted with and supposedly committed to the oracles of God.

We even see this irreverence displayed in Adam's transgression. He listened to the wisdom of the serpent, "For God knows that in the day you eat of it your eyes will be opened, and you will be like God, knowing good and evil" (Gen. 3:5).

"O God, who is like You?" the psalmist asks (Ps. 71:19), so it was futile for Adam to think that he could ever be *like God* apart from God. In the vanity of his mind, Adam reduced God to the level of mere man.

If you look at the wilderness error of the children of Israel, you will find the same root as the cause of their rebellion. Their fear of God was shaped by their own erroneous image of His glory.

Moses climbed Mount Sinai to receive the word of God. A number of days passed, so "the people gathered together" (Exod. 32:1). Problems always begin when people gather together in their own wisdom apart from God's power and presence. Instead of waiting as God commands us, people gather together and attempt to do something to satisfy themselves. What only God can provide is substituted with a temporary counterfeit.

They had seen God's power manifested time and again, yet they formed a calf of gold. Today this may seem ridiculous, but it wasn't so ridiculous for the Israelites. For over four hundred years, the Israelites had seen such objects in Egypt. It was a familiar part of the Egyptian culture and therefore common.

Once formed, the calf of gold was brought before the people, who, with one accord, said, "This is your god, O Israel, that brought you out of the land of Egypt!" (Exod. 32:4). Then a proclamation was made by their leader: "Tomorrow is a feast to the Lord" (Exod. 32:5). To understand what they were saying we must look at the Hebrew word for "Lord" in verse 5. It is the word *Yehovah,* also known as *Jehovah* or *Yahweh.* This word is defined as "the Existing One," the proper name of the one true God.

They used the name of the only true God. This was the name of the One whom Moses preached, the name of the One with whom Abraham had a covenant, the name of the One whom we serve. Jehovah is not used to describe any false gods in the Bible. This name of Jehovah or *Yahweh* was so sacred that later the Hebrew scribes were not permitted to write the word in full; they intentionally omitted the vowels in reverence to the name's sacredness.

So in essence the people, leaders as well, had pointed to this golden calf and called it Jehovah, the one true God, who had delivered them out of Egypt! They did not say, "This is Baal, the one who delivered you out of Egypt," nor did they use any other false god's name. They called this calf the name of the Lord, thus

14

reducing the greatness of the Lord to the common terms and finite images they were so familiar with.

It is interesting to note that the Israelites still acknowledged that it was Jehovah who delivered them from their bondage. They did not deny He did it; they just reduced God's greatness to a level they were more accustomed to dealing with. In the Old Testament, coming out of Egypt is a type of coming out of the world and being saved as taught in the New Testament. The Old Testament's natural happenings are types and shadows of what was to come in the New Testament.

SERVING GOD IN THE IMAGES WE HAVE MADE

NOW HEAR what Paul writes to us in the New Testament:

> For since the creation of the world His invisible attributes are clearly seen, being understood by the things that are made, even His eternal power and Godhead, so that they are without excuse, because, although they knew God, they did not glorify Him as God, nor were thankful.
> —ROMANS 1:20–21

Notice they do not glorify Him as God. The children of Israel acknowledged the deliverance of Jehovah, but they did not give Him the honor, reverence, or glory He deserved. Well, it hasn't changed much, for look what Paul goes on to say about these people living in New Testament times, who do not give God the reverence deserved:

> . . . and changed the glory of the incorruptible God into an image made like corruptible man.
> —ROMANS 1:23

Again we see the one true God's glorious image reduced. This time it is not to a calf but rather to the image of corruptible man. Israel was surrounded by a society that worshiped golden images in the likenesses of animals and insects. The modern-day church is surrounded by a culture that worships man.

For the past several years this statement has run through my mind on a consistent basis:

We have served God in the image we have made.

In my travels to hundreds of churches, I have encountered a mindset that reduces the image and glory of God to the image of mere corruptible man. This mentality permeates the church.

There are people who are quick to acknowledge Jesus as Savior, Healer, and Deliverer. With their mouths they acknowledge His lordship. Yet they reduce His glory to the level of corruptible man by their actions and heart attitudes.

They say, "God is my Friend; He understands my heart." It is true that God does understand our hearts even more thoroughly than we can understand ourselves. But usually this comment is given in justification of actions that contradict His covenant. The fact is, they are in disobedience to God's Word. In the Scriptures, the only people I see God calling His friends are those who tremble at His Word and presence and are quick to obey, no matter the cost.

Therefore, He does not receive the honor and reverence He deserves, or else they would instantly obey Him. With their lips they honor Him, but their fear toward Him is taught by the commandments of men. They have filtered God's Word and commands through their own culturally influenced thinking. Their image of His glory is formed by their limited perceptions rather than by His true image as revealed through His living Word.

This sets these men and women up to be quick to criticize authority, as our society is so quick to do. We have television programming from sitcoms to talk shows that constantly rail against authority. Media mock leadership and exalt the devious and rebellious. But what if the leadership is actually corrupt? What does God say concerning this? He says, "You shall not speak evil of a ruler of your people" (Acts 23:5). Yet we assume God approves of criticizing corrupt leadership because we've reduced His response to the level of our society, processing Him down to the image of corruptible man, even in our churches.

I have heard church leaders justify a divorce with, "God wants me to be happy." They actually believe their happiness takes precedence over their obedience to God's Word and the covenant they made with Him.

One church leader told me, "John, I have decided to divorce my mate because we just haven't gotten along for the past eighteen years. We don't watch movies together or do fun things together. You know I love Jesus, and if I am not doing the right thing, He will show me." Why would God grant us a private audience with Him when we ignore what He has already declared?

Somehow these individuals have distorted the words of Jesus to justify an exception for them. It's as if He has said, "When I said in My Word that I hated divorce, that didn't apply to you. I want you to be happy and have a mate that will do fun things with you. Go ahead and get divorced. If it's wrong you can repent later."

That's the way our society thinks. Our unspoken words declare, "There is black-and-white for others, but it's gray for me. It's wrong for others because it doesn't affect me, but I'm exempt if obeying makes my life uncomfortable!"

When this is done on a personal level, it will be done on a corporate level as well. So it is not surprising that in the church God's glory is reduced to corruptible man's degree—from the personal lives of church leadership right down to the messages preached from the pulpit.

What sort of message does this reduction of God's glory send to the congregation? It says, "God does not mean or do what He says." Then we wonder why sin runs rampant among us and the fear of God is lost. It is no wonder that sinners sit passively in our pews unconvicted by our preaching. It is no wonder lukewarmness is prevalent in our "Bible-based churches." It is no wonder that widows, orphans, incarcerated men and women, and the sick are neglected by believers.

Often the messages we've preached over the past twenty years via pulpits and airwaves have given God the appearance of the "Sugar Daddy in the sky" whose desire is to give us whatever we want, whenever we want it. This spawns short-lived obedience for selfish reasons. Parents who raise their children in this manner end up with spoiled children. Spoiled children lack a true respect for authority, especially when they do not get *what they want when they want it.* Their lack of reverence for authority sets them up to be easily offended with God.

How can we see reverence restored when we have fallen so short of His glory? How can obedience prevail when disobedience and rebellion are considered normal? God will restore His holy fear to His people and turn them back to Him that they might give Him the true glory and honor He is so worthy of receiving. He has promised, "But truly, as I live, all the earth shall be filled with the glory of the Lord" (Num. 14:21).

THE MORE EXTENSIVE
OUR COMPREHENSION OF
GOD'S GREATNESS . . . THE
GREATER OUR CAPACITY FOR FEAR
OR REVERENCE OF HIM.

Three

THE SERMON
OF THE UNIVERSE

*My soul thirsts for You; My flesh longs for You . . . to see Your power
and Your glory.*

—PSALM 63:1–2

I N ORDER to give God due reverence we must pursue the
knowledge of the greatness of His glory. This was the heart
cry of Moses when he boldly pleaded, "Please, show me Your
glory" (Exod. 33:18).

The more extensive our comprehension of God's greatness
(though in itself it is incomprehensible) the greater our capacity
for fear or reverence of Him. For this reason the psalmist encourages us, "For God is the King of all the earth; sing praises
with understanding" (Ps. 47:7). We are invited to behold His
greatness.

Yet we are also quickly told by the psalmist, "Great is the
Lord, and greatly to be praised; and His greatness is unsearch-
able" (Ps. 145:3). This causes me to recall the story of St.
Augustine's death. Augustine was one of the greatest leaders in
his era. His writings expounded on the awesome wonders of our
God. His writings have been referenced for over a thousand

years. One of his great works is entitled *The City of God.*

On his deathbed, surrounded by his closest friends, as Augustine slipped away to be with the Lord, his breath ceased, and his heart stopped, and a wonderful sense of peace filled the room. Suddenly his eyes reopened, and with his face aglow he declared to those present, "I have seen the Lord. All I have written is but straw." Then he left for his eternal home.

HOLY, HOLY, HOLY . . .

ISAIAH HAD a vision of the unsearchable glory of God. He saw the Lord in His throne room, high and lifted up, and His glory filled the room. Around Him stood massive angels called seraphim, who, because of God's great glory, cover their faces with their wings and cry out:

> "Holy, holy, holy is the Lord of hosts; The whole earth is full of His glory!"
>
> —ISAIAH 6:3

We have sung these exact words in our churches in hymn form. Yet most often our praises ring void of the passion found in these angels. You will most likely see people yawning or glancing about as they sing the words. Oh, how different is the atmosphere in God's throne room!

These mighty, awesome angels are not bored or restless; they are not merely singing nice songs. They do not say, "God, I have been singing this song before Your throne for millions of years; do You think a replacement could be brought in? I would like to go explore the other parts of heaven." No way! They would not desire to be anywhere else but crying out and singing praises before the throne of God.

These spectacular angels are not merely singing a song. They are responding to what they see. Every moment, through veiled eyes they glimpse another facet and a greater dimension of God's glory being revealed. Overwhelmed, they shout, "Holy, holy, holy!" In fact, their combined cry is so loud that the posts of the door are shaken by their voices and the entire room is filled with smoke. Wow, it's one thing for sound waves to shake a natural building here on the earth, but it is quite another matter to shake the doorposts of heaven's architecture! These angels have been around God's throne for untold ages, for time immeasurable. Yet they experience a perpetual revelation of God's power and wisdom. His greatness is truly unsearchable.

HIS WORKS SPEAK OF HIS GLORY

IN THE LAST chapter, we learned of man's great folly—reducing the glory of the Lord to our image and to the measure of corruptible man. We saw this evidenced to an alarming degree in the church. The rest of this chapter will be devoted to glimpsing just a bit of God's glory as it is revealed in His creation. Let's look beyond the technical and meditate on the wonder of what is described, for His creation preaches quite a sermon and gives us points to ponder.

Psalm 145:10–11 says, "All Your works shall praise You, O Lord . . . they shall speak of the glory of Your kingdom, and talk of Your power."

I have four sons. There was a period of time when my sons were a little too interested in a certain professional basketball player. He is one of the most popular athletes in America, and idolized by many in this nation. The NBA playoffs were in full swing. I heard this player's name continually brought up by the press, by my sons, and by their friends.

I was with my family ministering on the Atlantic coast. We had just come in from the beach where the boys had tumbled and danced in the waves. As we dried off after our swim, I sat down with my three oldest boys for a talk with dad.

Pointing out the window, I questioned them. "Boys, that's a massive ocean out there, isn't it?"

In unison, they answered, "Yeah, dad."

I continued, "You can only see about one or two miles of it, but the ocean actually goes on for thousands of miles."

Wrapped in the warmth and safety of towels, the boys listened with wide eyes. "Wow!"

"And this one isn't even the biggest ocean; there is another even bigger one called the Pacific Ocean. Then there are two more besides it."

The boys all nodded in silent wonder as they listened to the power of the pounding surf now at high tide outside our window.

Knowing that to some degree my sons had grasped the overwhelming amount of water I had just described, I asked, "Boys, do you know God weighed all the water that you see, and all that I have just described, in the palm of His hand?" (See Isaiah 40:12.)

Their mouths and eyes registered genuine amazement. They had been impressed because this famous sports figure could palm a basketball! Now holding a basketball in one hand would seem insignificant.

"Do you know what else the Bible says about how great God is?" I asked.

"What, Dad?"

"The Bible declares God can measure the universe with the span of His hand" (Isa. 40:12). Holding my own hand before them, I demonstrated that a span was the distance from the tip of my thumb to the tip of my pinkie. "God can measure the universe in the distance from His thumb to the tip of His smallest finger!"

THE NEVER-ENDING SERMON

THE VERY universe declares the glory of the Lord. Read the inspired writings of David:

> The heavens declare the glory of God; the skies proclaim the work of his hands. Day after day they pour forth speech; night after night they display knowledge. There is no speech or language where their voice is not heard. Their voice goes out into all the earth, their words to the ends of the world.
>
> —PSALM 19:1–4, NIV

Pause for a moment and ponder the boundless expanse of the universe. Do so and you will catch a fleeting glimpse of His unlimited glory! In the words of David, "The universe declares it." God's creation is not limited to the earth but encompasses even the unknown universe. He arranged the stars of the heavens with His fingers. (See Psalm 8:3.) For most of us, it is difficult to comprehend the vastness of the universe.

Beside our sun, the nearest star is 4.3 light years away. So that this number does not remain just a figure, let's expound on it. Light travels at the speed of 186,282 miles per second—not per hour but per second. That is roughly 670,000,000 miles per hour. Our airplanes fly approximately 500 miles per hour.

The moon orbits roughly 239,000 miles from the earth. If we traveled by plane to the moon, it would take nineteen days. But light reaches there in 1.3 seconds!

Let's continue. The sun is 93,000,000 miles from the earth. If you boarded a jumbo jet today and traveled to the sun, your journey would take over twenty-one years! That's nonstop too! Where were you twenty-one years ago? That's a long time. Can you imagine flying that long without a moment's break in order to reach the sun? For those who prefer driving . . . well, it couldn't be done in a lifetime. It would take roughly two hundred years, not including any gas or rest stops! Yet light travels this distance in a mere eight minutes and twenty seconds!

Let's leave the sun and move on to the nearest star. We already know it is 4.3 light years from the earth. If we built a scale model of the earth, sun, and nearest star, it would be as follows. In proportion, the earth would reduce to the size of a peppercorn, and the sun would become the size of an eight-inch-diameter ball. According to this size scale, the distance from the earth to the sun would be twenty-six yards, which is only a quarter the length of a football field. Yet remember, for a scale airplane to span that twenty-six-yard distance, it would take more than twenty-one years.

So if this is the earth's and sun's ratio, can you guess how far the nearest star would be to our peppercorn earth? Would you think a thousand yards, two thousand, or maybe a mile? Not even close. Our nearest star would be placed four thousand miles away from the peppercorn! That means if you put the peppercorn earth in San Diego, California, the nearest star on our scale model would be positioned past New York City and into the Atlantic Ocean a thousand miles out to sea!

To reach this closest star by airplane would take approximately fifty-one billion years, non-stop! That's 51,000,000,000 years! Yet light from this star travels to earth in only 4.3 years!

Let's expand further. The stars you see at night with the naked eye are one hundred to one thousand light years away. However, there are a few stars you can see with the naked eye that are four thousand light years away. I wouldn't even attempt to calculate the amount of time it would take for a plane to reach just one of these stars. But, think of it; light travels at a rate of 186,282 miles per second, and it still takes four thousand years to reach the earth. That means the light of these stars was first released before Moses parted the Red Sea, and has traveled a distance of six hundred seventy million miles every hour without slowing down or ceasing since, and is just now reaching the earth!

But these are only the stars in our galaxy. A galaxy is a vast gathering of usually billions of stars. The galaxy in which we live is called the Milky Way. So let's expound further.

The closest galaxy to ours is the Andromeda Galaxy. Its distance from us is approximately 2.31 million light years away! Imagine, over two million light years away! Have we reached the limit of our understanding yet?

Scientists estimate there are billions of galaxies, each of them loaded with billions of stars. Galaxies tend to group together. Andromeda Galaxy and our Milky Way are part of a cluster of at least thirty galaxies. Other clusters could contain as many as thousands of galaxies.

The Guinness Book of World Records states that in June 1994 a new group of cocoon-shaped clusters of galaxies was discovered. The distance across this group of galaxies was calculated at six hundred fifty million light years! Can you imagine how long it would take to cross such a vast distance by airplane?

The Guinness Book of World Records also states that the most remote object ever seen by man appears to be over 13.2 billion light years away. Our finite minds cannot even begin to comprehend distances this immense. We've yet to glimpse the ends of the galaxy clusters let alone the end of the universe. And God can measure all this with the span of His hand! To top it off, the psalmist tells us, "He [God] counts the number of the stars; He calls them all by name. Great is our Lord, and mighty in power; His understanding is infinite" (Ps. 147:4–5). Not only can He count the billions upon billions of stars, but He knows the name of each one! No wonder the psalmist exclaimed, "His understanding is infinite."

Solomon said, "But will God indeed dwell on the earth? Behold, heaven and the heaven of heavens cannot contain You" (1 Kings 8:27). Are you getting a greater glimpse of His glory?

HIS GLORIOUS WISDOM IS REVEALED IN CREATION

He has made the earth by His power, He has established the world by His wisdom. . . .

—JEREMIAH 10:12

Not only are the greatness and power of God's glory seen in creation but also His great wisdom and knowledge. Science has spent years and expended vast amounts of money to study the workings of this natural world. God's designs and building blocks remain a marvel.

All forms of created life are based on cells. Cells are the building blocks of the human body, plants, animals, and every other living thing. The human body, which in itself is an engineering wonder, contains about 100,000,000,000,000 cells—(Can you comprehend that number?)—of which there are a vast variety. In His wisdom, He designated these cells to perform specific tasks. They grow, multiply, and eventually die—right on schedule.

Though invisible to the naked eye, cells are not the smallest particles known to man. Cells consist of numerous tinier structures called molecules, and molecules are comprised of even smaller structures called elements—and within elements can be found even tinier structures called atoms.

Atoms are so small that the period at the end of this sentence contains more than a billion of them. As minute as an atom is, it is made up almost entirely of empty space. The rest of the atom is composed of protons, neutrons, and electrons. Protons and neutrons are found clustered together in a minuscule and extremely dense nucleus at the very center of the atom. Little bundles of energy called electrons whiz around this nucleus at the speed of light. These are the core building blocks that hold all things together.

So where does the atom get its energy? And what force holds its energetic particles together? Scientists call it atomic energy. This is merely a scientific term to describe what they cannot explain. For God has already said He is "upholding all things by the word of His power" (Heb. 1:3). Colossians 1:17 says, "In him all things hold together" (NIV).

Stop and ponder this for just a moment. Here is this glorious Maker whom even the universe cannot contain. The universe is measured by the span of His hand, yet He is so detailed in His design of the tiny earth and His creatures that it leaves modern science baffled after years of study.

Now you can more clearly understand the psalmist when he states: "I will praise You, for I am fearfully and wonderfully made" (Ps. 139:14). You can also see, especially in this dispensation with all the scientific knowledge we have amassed to date, why the Word says, "The fool has said in his heart, 'There is no God'" (Ps. 14:1).

Of course, many books can be written on the wonders and wisdom of His creation. That is not my intent here. My purpose is to awaken amazement and wonder at the works of His hands, for they declare His great glory!

"WE SEE IT, DAD!"

BACK TO THE incident with my boys. After relating all this scientific information in terms they could understand, I concluded, "So you are impressed with a man who can jump from the fifteen-foot-line on a basketball court and put a ball filled with air into a little hoop?"

They said, "We see it, dad!"

"What does this basketball player have that God did not give him?" I concluded.

They answered, "Nothing!"

Since then, their opinion of this man has changed from hero worship to healthy respect. In fact, their basketball cards are now called "prayer cards." They are praying for the salvation of these men whom others see as heroes.

You can understand a little better now what God was really saying when He asked Job, "Who has preceded Me, that I should pay him? Everything under heaven is Mine" (Job 41:11).

WHAT IS MAN?

> When I consider your heavens, the work of your fingers, the moon and the stars, which you have set in place, what is man that you are mindful of him, the son of man that you care for him?
>
> —PSALM 8:3–4, NIV

I believe, though I cannot prove this, that Psalm 8 records the response at creation of one of the mighty seraphim angels that surround the throne of God. Stop and think of this and try to see through this angel's eyes. This awesome, mighty God, who has just created the universe and put the stars in place with His fingers, now comes to a little speck of a planet called earth, and makes what appears to be a tiny insignificant speck of dust into the body of a man.

But what really amazes this angel is God's total focus of attention. It's fixed entirely on this being called man. We are told by the psalmist that His thoughts toward us are precious, and that the sum of them is so great that if they were counted, it would be more than the sand on the earth (Ps. 139:17–18). In seeing this, I believe this angel cries out, "What is this that You are so interested in and fondly affectionate toward? What is that little thing that is constantly on Your mind—the total focus of Your plans?"

Take the time, be still, and consider the works of His hands. We are told to do this. As you do, creation will preach a sermon to you. It will declare His glory!

BEFORE GOD'S GLORY
COMES, THERE FIRST MUST
BE DIVINE ORDER.

Four

ORDER, GLORY, JUDGMENT: PART I

For it is the God who commanded light to shine out of darkness, who has shone in our hearts to give the light of the knowledge of the glory of God in the face of Jesus Christ.

—2 CORINTHIANS 4:6

I N THE NEXT few chapters we'll establish an important pattern that occurs throughout the Scriptures. It will become the historical framework that supports the issues that pertain to today.

GOD'S PATTERN

IT WAS THE FIRST night of four scheduled meetings in Saskatchewan, Canada. The pastor was in the process of introducing me, and I would be on the platform in just under three minutes.

Suddenly, the Spirit of God began to walk me quickly through the Bible, revealing a pattern occurring throughout the Old and New Testaments. The pattern is this:

1. Divine order

2. God's glory
3. Judgment

Before God manifests His glory, there must be divine order. Once His glory is revealed, there is great blessing. But also once His glory is revealed, any irreverence, disorder or disobedience is met with immediate judgment.

God had opened my eyes to this pattern in less than two minutes, and He let me know I was to preach it to the hungry congregation of Canadians before me. That evening was one of the most powerful services I had held, and I want to share it's truth with you.

FROM THE BEGINNING

TO LAY A foundation, let's go to the beginning. When God created the heavens and earth:

> The earth was without form, and void; and darkness was on the face of the deep. And the Spirit of God was hovering over the face of the waters.
>
> —GENESIS 1:2

The English words "without form" are a combination of the two Hebrew words, *hayah* and *tohuw*. Together these two words render a more descriptive account: "The earth became formless and chaotic." There was no order but *disorder*.

Though the Spirit of God hovered or brooded over this chaos, He would not move upon it until the Word of God was released. With God's spoken words, divine order was set into operation on this planet. God prepared the earth for six days before He released His glory into it. He took special care with the garden He had planted for His own. Then God created His man—the focus of creation.

Once the garden was prepared, God "formed man of the dust of the ground." Science has found every chemical element of the human body resident in the earth's crust. God designed both an

34

engineering and a scientific wonder.

DIVINE ORDER BRINGS GOD'S GLORY

GOD SPENT SIX days bringing divine order to the earth. Then He brought order into man's body. Once divine order was achieved, God "breathed into his nostrils the breath of life; and man became a living being" (Gen. 2:7). God literally breathed His Spirit into this human body.

Man was created in the image and likeness of God, and then woman was taken from the side of man. Neither had clothing or a covering. "And they were both naked, the man and his wife, and were not ashamed" (Gen. 2:25). All other creatures were given coverings. Animals have fur, birds have feathers, fish have scales or shells. But man did not need an outer covering, for the psalmist tells us God "crowned him with glory and honor" (Ps. 8:5). The Hebrew word for "crowned" is *atar.* It means "to encircle or surround." In essence, the man and woman were clothed with the glory of the Lord and didn't need natural clothing.

The blessings this first couple experienced were indescribable. The garden yielded its strength without having to cultivate it. The animals were in harmony with the man. There were no sicknesses, diseases, or poverty. But best of all, this couple had the privilege of walking with God in His glory!

JUDGMENT

GOD FIRST brought divine order by His Word and Spirit. Then His glory was revealed. Blessing abounded, but then came the fall. The Lord God commanded the man not to eat of the fruit of the tree of the knowledge of good and evil, for to disobey would be immediate spiritual death.

Mocking God, Satan challenged God's Word with his twisted contradiction, "You will not surely die. For God knows the day you eat of it your eyes will be opened, and you will be like God, knowing good and evil" (Gen. 3:4–5). Then Adam, with full knowledge of his actions, chose to disobey God. His irreverence was nothing less than high treason. When this happened, judgment followed.

At once Adam and Eve knew they were naked. The glory had departed, leaving them uncovered and separated from God in a state of spiritual death. In a futile attempt to cover their nakedness, they hastily prepared a few leaves and vines and clothed themselves by the work of their hands. God saw what they had done, pronounced judgment upon them, and clothed them in tunics of skins, most likely from a lamb, foreshadowing the Lamb of God who would come and restore man's relationship with God. Then the fallen couple was driven from the garden where eternal life was found. Judgment was severe—the result of Adam's irreverent disobedience in the presence of God's glory.

THE TABERNACLE OF HIS GLORY

SEVERAL HUNDRED years pass, and God finally finds a friend in Abram. God makes a covenant of promise with Abram and changes his name to *Abraham*. Through this man's obedience, the promises of God are once again secured for generations to come. Abraham's descendants end up in Egypt as slaves for more than four hundred years. In their hardship God raises up a prophet and deliverer named Moses.

Once the descendants of Abraham are delivered out of bondage, God brings them into the wilderness. It is in the wilderness of Mount Sinai that God outlines His plan to dwell with His people. God tells Moses, "I am the Lord their God, who brought them up out of the land of Egypt, that I may dwell among them" (Exod. 29:46).

Once again God will walk with man, for this has always been His desire. Yet because of man's fallen state, God cannot dwell within him. So He instructs Moses, "Let them make Me a sanctuary, that I may dwell among them" (Exod. 25:8). This sanctuary was called the tabernacle.

Before God's glory comes, there first must be divine order. Therefore, God carefully instructs Moses how to build the tabernacle. He is very specific on all points of who is to build it and who is to serve in it. These instructions are detailed in their materials, measurements, furnishings, and offerings. In fact, the specific instructions fill many chapters in the Book of Exodus.

This man-made sanctuary reflected the heavenly one (Heb. 9:23–24). God warned Moses, "See that you make all things according to the pattern shown you on the mountain" (Heb. 8:5; see also Exod. 25:40). It was of extreme importance that all was done exactly as shown. This would provide the divine order necessary before the King's glory would be manifested in their presence.

An offering was received from the congregation that supplied all the materials they needed—gold, silver, bronze, blue, purple, and scarlet threads, fine linen, skins, fur, acacia wood, oil, spices, and precious stones.

The Lord had told Moses, "See, I have called by name Bezalel . . . of the tribe of Judah. And I have filled him with the Spirit of God, in wisdom, in understanding, in knowledge, and in all manner of workmanship . . . And I, indeed I, have appointed with him Aholiab the son of Ahisamach, of the tribe of Dan; and I have put wisdom in the hearts of all who are gifted artisans, that they may make all that I have commanded you" (Exod. 31:1–3, 6). God's Spirit was on these men to bring divine order. The Spirit of God working through men, joined in harmony with God's Word, would once again bring about divine order.

Then all these skilled men began work on the tabernacle. They made the curtains, screens, and poles. They forged the ark of the testimony, the table for the showbread, the gold lamp stand, the altar of incense, the altar of burnt offering, the bronze laver. They made the priestly garments and the anointing oil.

> According to all that the Lord had commanded Moses, so the children of Israel did all the work. Then Moses looked over all the work, and indeed they had done it; as the Lord had commanded, just so they had done it. And Moses blessed them.

> Then the Lord spoke to Moses, saying, "On the first day
> of the first month you shall set up the tabernacle of the
> tent of meeting."
>
> —EXODUS 39:42–40:2

God's instructions were so specific that the tabernacle had to
be erected on this exact day.

The first day of the first month arrived. Moses and the skilled
artisans raised the tabernacle. Then we read:

> So Moses finished the work.
>
> —EXODUS 40:33

Everything was ready now. Divine order was in place by the
Word of God and a people submitted to the leading of the Holy
Spirit. Now notice what happens:

> Then the cloud covered the tabernacle of meeting, and the
> glory of the Lord filled the tabernacle. And Moses was not
> able to enter the tabernacle of meeting, because the cloud
> rested above it, and the glory of the Lord filled the taber-
> nacle.
>
> —EXODUS 40:34–35

Once divine order was attained God revealed His glory. Most
of us in the church lack an understanding of the glory of the
Lord. I have attended many meetings where ministers have
declared, either out of ignorance or hype, "The glory of the Lord
is here." Before we proceed further, let's discuss what the glory of
the Lord is.

THE GLORY OF THE LORD

FIRST OF ALL, the glory of the Lord is not a cloud. Some may
ask, "Then why is a cloud mentioned almost every time God's
glory is manifested in Scriptures?" The reason: God hides
Himself in the cloud. He is too magnificent for mankind to

behold. If the cloud did not screen out His countenance, all around Him would be consumed and immediately die.

> And he [Moses] said, "Please, show me Your glory." But He [God] said, "You cannot see My face; for no man shall see Me, and live."
>
> —EXODUS 33:18–20

Mortal flesh cannot stand in the presence of the Holy Lord in His glory. Paul says:

> He who is the blessed and only Potentate, the King of kings and Lord of lords, who alone has immortality, dwelling in unapproachable light, whom no man has seen or can see, to whom be honor and everlasting power. Amen.
>
> —1 TIMOTHY 6:15–16

Hebrews 12:29 tells us that God is a consuming fire. Now when you think of this do not consider a wood fire. A consuming fire could not be contained in the confines of your fireplace. "God is light and in Him is no darkness at all" (1 John 1:5). The type of fire that burns in your fireplace does not produce perfect light. It contains darkness. It is approachable and you can look at it.

So let's move on to a more intense light. Consider the laser beam. It is a very focused and intense light but it is still not perfect light. As bright and powerful as it is, there is darkness in laser light also.

Let's consider the sun. The sun is enormous and unapproachable, bright and powerful, but it still contains darkness within the fire of its light.

Paul says to Timothy that His glory is "unapproachable light, whom no man has seen or can see."

Paul could very easily write this because he experienced a measure of this light on the road to Damascus. He related it this way to King Agrippa:

> At midday, O king, along the road I saw a light from
> heaven, brighter than the sun, shining around me.
>
> —ACTS 26:13

Paul said this light was brighter than the noonday sun! Take a
moment and try to look directly at the midday sun. It is difficult
to look at the sun unless it is veiled with a cloud. God in His
glory exceeds this brilliance many fold.

Paul did not see the Lord's face; he only saw the light ema-
nating from Him, for he had to ask, "Who are You, Lord?" He
could not see His form or the features of His face, he was so
blinded by the light that emanated from His glory, overwhelming even the brightness of the Middle Eastern sun!

Perhaps this explains why both the prophets Joel and Isaiah
stated that in the last days when the glory of the Lord is revealed
the sun will be turned into darkness. "Behold, the day of the
Lord comes . . . the stars of heaven and their constellations will
not give their light; the sun will be darkened in its going forth,
and the moon will not cause its light to shine" (Isa. 13:9–10).

God's glory will overcome all other light. He is the perfect and
all consuming light. "They shall go into the holes of the rocks,
and into the caves of the earth, from the terror of the Lord and
the glory of His majesty, when He arises to shake the earth
mightily" (Isa. 2:19).

God's glory is so overpowering that when He came before the
children of Israel in the midst of the dark cloud at Sinai, the
people cried out in terror and drew back. Moses describes it:

> The Lord spoke to all your assembly, in the mountain from
> the midst of the fire, the cloud, and the thick darkness,
> with a loud voice . . . So it was, when you heard the voice
> from the midst of the darkness, while the mountain was
> burning with fire, that you came near to me, all the heads
> of your tribes and your elders.
>
> And you said: "Surely the Lord our God has shown us
> His glory and His greatness, and we have heard His voice
> from the midst of the fire. We have seen this day that God

40

speaks with man; yet he still lives. Now therefore, why should we die? For this great fire will consume us; if we hear the voice of the Lord our God anymore, then we shall die."

—DEUTERONOMY 5:22–27

Though they saw Him shrouded in the thick darkness of a cloud it could not hide the brilliance of His glory.

ALL THAT MAKES GOD, GOD

SO NOW LET'S ask the question, *What is the glory of the Lord?* In answer, we return to Moses' request on the mountain of God. Moses asked:

Please, show me Your glory.

—EXODUS 33:18

The Hebrew word for "glory" used by Moses in this instance was *kabowd*. It is defined by *Strong's Bible Dictionary* as "the weight of something, but only figuratively in a good sense." Its definition also speaks of splendor, abundance, and honor. Moses was asking, "Show me Yourself in *all* your splendor." Look carefully at God's response:

Then He said, "I will make all My goodness pass before you, and I will proclaim the name of the Lord before you."

—EXODUS 33:19

Moses requested all His glory, and God referred to it as, "all My *goodness*..." The Hebrew word for "goodness" is *tuwb*. It means, "good in the widest sense." In other words, nothing is withheld.

Then God says, "I will proclaim the name of the Lord before you." Before an earthly king enters the throne room, his name is always announced by proclamation. Then he enters in his splendor. The king's greatness is revealed, and in his court there is no mistake as to who is king. If this monarch were on the street of one of the cities of his nation dressed in ordinary clothes, without any attendants, he might be passed by without those around him realizing his actual identity. So in essence, this is exactly what God did for Moses. He is saying, "I will proclaim My own name and pass by you in all My splendor."

We see then that the glory of the Lord is everything that makes God, God. All His characteristics, authority, power, wisdom—literally the immeasurable weight and magnitude of God—are contained within God's glory. Nothing is hidden or held back!

HIS GLORY IS REVEALED IN CHRIST

WE ARE TOLD that the glory of the Lord is revealed in the face of Jesus Christ (2 Cor. 4:6). Many have claimed to have seen a vision of Jesus and looked upon His face. That is very possible. Paul described it, "For now we see through a glass, darkly; but then face to face" (1 Cor. 13:12, KJV). His glory is veiled by darkened glass, for no man can look upon His fully unveiled glory and live.

Someone else may question, "But the disciples looked at the face of Jesus after He rose from the dead!" That too is correct. The reason it is true is that He did not openly display His glory. There were some who saw the Lord, even in the Old Testament, but He was not revealed in His glory. The Lord appeared to Abraham by the terebinth trees of Mamre (Gen. 18:1–2). Joshua looked at the face of the Lord before invading Jericho (Josh. 5:13–14). The Lord said to him, "Take your sandal off your foot, for the place where you stand is holy" (v. 15).

The same is true after the Resurrection. The disciples ate a fish breakfast with Jesus at the Sea of Tiberias (John 21:9–10). Two disciples walked with Jesus on the road to Emmaus, "but their eyes were restrained" (Luke 24:16). These all beheld His face because He did not openly display His glory.

In contrast, John the Apostle saw the Lord in the Spirit and had a totally different encounter than breakfast with Him by the sea, for John saw Him in His glory:

> I was in the Spirit on the Lord's Day, and I heard behind me a loud voice, as of a trumpet . . . Then I turned to see the voice that spoke with me. And having turned I saw seven golden lampstands, and in the midst of the seven lampstands One like the Son of Man, clothed with a garment down to the feet and girded about the chest with a golden band. His head and hair were white like wool, as white as snow, and His eyes like a flame of fire; His feet were like fine brass, as if refined in a furnace, and His voice as the sound of many waters; He had in His right hand seven stars, out of His mouth went a sharp two-edged sword, and His countenance was like the sun shining in its strength. And when I saw Him, I fell at His feet as dead.
> —REVELATION 1:10; 12–17

Notice, His countenance was like the sun shining in its strength. How then could John look at Him? The reason: He was in the Spirit, just as Isaiah was in the Spirit when he saw the throne and the seraphim above it and the One who sat on it (Isa. 6:1–4). Moses could not look upon God's face, for Moses was in his natural physical body.

HE HAS WITHHELD
HIS GLORY TO TEST US

THE GLORY of the Lord is all that makes up God. This far surpasses our ability to comprehend and understand, for even the mighty seraphim continue to cry, "Holy, holy, holy . . . " in awe and overwhelming wonder.

The four living creatures before His throne cry, "Holy, holy, holy, Lord God Almighty, Who was and is and is to come!" (Rev. 4:8).

> Whenever the living creatures give glory and honor and thanks to Him who sits on the throne, who lives forever and ever, the twenty-four elders fall down before Him who sits on the throne and worship Him who lives forever and

ever, and cast their crowns before the throne, saying: "You are worthy, O Lord, to receive glory and honor and power; for You created all things, and by Your will they exist and were created."

—REVELATION 4:9–10

He deserves more glory than any living created being can give Him throughout eternity!

We must remember, we serve the One who created the universe and the earth. He is from everlasting and will be to everlasting! There is no other like Him. In His wisdom, He purposely withholds the revelation of His glory to see if we will serve Him with love and reverence, or turn our attention to that which receives glory on the earth yet pales in comparison to Him.

WE CANNOT EXPECT
TO BE ADMITTED INTO HIS
PRESENCE WITH AN ATTITUDE
OF DISRESPECT.

Five

ORDER, GLORY, JUDGMENT: PART II

The priests could not continue ministering because of the cloud; for the glory of the Lord filled the house of God.
—2 CHRONICLES 5:14

ONCE THE tabernacle was erected, divine order was achieved. As soon as everything was in place:

> Then the cloud covered the tabernacle of meeting, and the glory of the Lord filled the tabernacle. And Moses was not able to enter the tabernacle of meeting, because the cloud rested above it, and the glory of the Lord filled the tabernacle.
> —EXODUS 40:34–35

After our discussion on the glory of the Lord we can understand why even God's friend, Moses, could not enter in. The tabernacle was permeated with the glory of the Lord!

God's glory manifesting and abiding among Israel brought tremendous blessing. In His glorious presence were provision, guidance, healing, and protection. No enemy could stand before Israel. The revelation of His Word was abundant. There was also the benefit of having the cloud of His glory to shade the children of Israel from the heat of the desert by day, as well as to provide warmth and light for them at night. There was no lack of anything they needed.

JUDGMENT

GOD HAD previously instructed Moses, "Now take Aaron your brother, and his sons with him, from among the children of Israel, that he may minister to Me as priest, Aaron and Aaron's sons: Nadab, Abihu, Eleazar, and Ithamar" (Exod. 28:1).

These men were set apart and trained to minister to the Lord and stand in the gap for the people. Their duties and parameters for worship were outlined in very specific instructions passed on from God to Moses. Their training was a part of divine order. Following this instruction and training came the actual consecration of these men. With everything in place, their ministry began.

Read carefully what two of these priests did after the glory of the Lord had been revealed in the tabernacle:

> Nadab and Abihu, the sons of Aaron, each took his censer and put fire in it, put incense on it, and offered profane fire before the Lord, which He had not commanded them.
> —LEVITICUS 10:1

Notice Nadab and Abihu offered *profane* fire before the presence of the Lord. One definition for "profane" in *Webster's Dictionary* is:

> *Showing disrespect or contempt for sacred things; irreverent.*

It means to treat what God calls holy or sacred as if it were common. These two men grabbed the censers that were set apart for the worship of the Lord and filled them with the fire and incense of their choosing, not the offering prescribed by God. They were careless with what God had called holy and exhibited a lack of reverence. They came with irreverence into the presence of the Lord, bearing an unacceptable offering. They treated what was holy as common. Look what happens as a result:

> So fire went out from the Lord and devoured them, and they died before the Lord.
>
> —LEVITICUS 10:2

These two men were instantly judged for their irreverence. They were met with immediate death. Their irreverence took place after the revelation of God's glory. Though they were priests, they were not exempt from rendering God honor. They sinned by approaching a holy God as though He were common! They had become too familiar with His presence! Now hear the immediate words of Moses following this judgment of death.

> And Moses said to Aaron, "This is what the Lord spoke, saying: 'By those who come near Me I must be regarded as holy; and before all the people I must be glorified.'" So Aaron held his peace.
>
> —LEVITICUS 10:3

God had already made it clear that irreverence could not survive in the presence of a holy God. God is not mocked. Today is no different; He is the same holy God. We cannot expect to be admitted into His presence with an attitude of disrespect.

Nadab and Abihu were Moses' nephews. But Moses knew better than to question God's judgment, for He knew God to be just. In fact, Moses warns Aaron and his two surviving sons not to even mourn them lest they die as well. This would have further dishonored the Lord, so the bodies of Nadah and Abihu were carried outside the camp and buried.

Once again, we see the pattern—divine order, God's revealed glory, then judgment for irreverence.

A NEW SANCTUARY

ALMOST FIVE hundred years later, King David's son, Solomon, began a temple for the presence of the Lord. This was a massive undertaking. The store of materials, most of which were gathered under the reign of David, was enormous.

Before his death, David instructed Solomon:

> I have worked hard to provide materials for building the Temple of the Lord—nearly four thousand tons of gold, nearly forty thousand tons of silver, and so much iron and bronze that it cannot be weighed. I have also gathered lumber and stone for the walls, though you may need to add more.
>
> You have many skilled stonemasons and carpenters and craftsmen of every kind available to you. They are expert goldsmiths and silversmiths and workers of bronze and iron. Now begin the work, and may the Lord be with you!
>
> —1 CHRONICLES 22:14–16, NLT

Solomon added to the materials already provided and began the temple in the fourth year of his reign. The design of the temple was magnificent, its ornamentation and detail extraordinary. Even with a task force of tens of thousands of men, the gathering of materials and construction still took seven full years. We then read:

> So all the work that Solomon had done for the house of the Lord was finished.
>
> —2 CHRONICLES 5:1

Solomon then gathered Israel to Jerusalem where the temple stood. "Then the priests brought in the ark of the covenant of the Lord to its place" (2 Chron. 5:7). All the priests sanctified themselves. There would be no irreverence in the presence of God. They remembered the fate of their distant relatives, Nadab and Abihu.

Then the Levites who were the singers and musicians stood at the east end of the altar, clothed in white linen, and with them were one hundred and twenty priests, sounding with trumpets.

Once again, great care, time, and an enormous amount of work and preparation brought divine order. And what came after divine order? Let's read:

> Indeed it came to pass, when the trumpeters and singers were as one, to make one sound to be heard in praising and thanking the Lord, and when they lifted up their voice with the trumpets and cymbals and instruments of music, and praised the Lord, saying: "For He is good, for His mercy endures forever," that the house, the house of the Lord, was filled with a cloud, so that the priests could not continue ministering because of the cloud; for the glory of the Lord filled the house of God.
>
> —2 CHRONICLES 5:13–14

When divine order was achieved, the glory of the Lord was revealed. Again it was so overwhelming that the priests were unable to minister for the glory of the Lord filled the temple.

JUDGMENT

FOLLOWING THE revelation of God's glory, we again see irreverence towards His presence and Word. Though the Israelites knew His will, their hearts grew careless toward what God calls sacred and holy.

> Moreover all the leaders of the priests and the people transgressed more and more, according to all the abominations of the nations, and defiled the house of the Lord which He had consecrated in Jerusalem. And the Lord God of their fathers sent warnings to them by His messengers, rising up early and sending them, because He had compassion on His people and on His dwelling place. But they mocked

the messengers of God, despised His words, and scoffed at His prophets.

—2 CHRONICLES 36:14–16

They ridiculed His messengers and disregarded their words of warning. The people mocked His prophets. I have seen the same evidence of a great lack of fear today.

Recently I ministered at a large church, preaching a strong message on obedience and the lordship of Jesus. The wife of one of our staff members had left the service with her baby and gone to the lobby where the service was airing on closed-circuit television. She overheard two women of the church discussing the sermon: "Who does he think he is? Turn him off!" they scoffed. *Where is the fear of the Lord?*

Israel and Judah suffered repeated judgment due to their lack of fear and respect for God's sacred presence and His Word. Their judgment climaxed when Abraham's descendants were carried off into Babylonian captivity. Read this account:

> But they mocked the messengers of God, despised His words, and scoffed at His prophets, until the wrath of the Lord arose against His people, till there was no remedy.
>
> Therefore He brought against them the king of the Chaldeans, who killed their young men with the sword in the house of their sanctuary, and had no compassion on young man or virgin, on the aged or the weak; He [God] gave them all into his hand.
>
> And all the articles from the house of God, great and small, the treasures of the house of the Lord, and the treasures of the king and of his leaders, all these he took to Babylon. Then they burned the house of God, broke down the wall of Jerusalem, burned all its palaces with fire, and destroyed all its precious possessions.
>
> —2 CHRONICLES 36:16–19

I want you to think carefully about what I am about to say. We have retraced three accounts—the garden, the tabernacle, and the temple. In every case the judgment was severe. Each resulted in death and destruction.

What is most sobering is the fact that we are not talking about people who had never experienced God's glory or His presence. These judgments were against those who not only had heard His Word, but had walked in His presence and experienced His glory!

Now that we have laid a foundation from the Old Testament, let's move forward into the days of the New Testament. We again discover some very sobering truths and some exciting insights!

JESUS MAKES IT CLEAR THAT
TO FOLLOW HIM, WE MUST FIRST
COUNT THE COST . . . THE PRICE
IS NOTHING SHORT OF
OUR LIVES.

Six

A New Sanctuary

For you are the temple of the living God. As God has said: "I will dwell in them and walk among them."

—2 Corinthians 6:16

UNDER THE Old Covenant God's glorious presence dwelled first in the tabernacle, then within the temple of Solomon.

Now God prepares to move into what was always His desired dwelling—a temple not made of stone, but the temple found in the hearts of His sons and daughters.

MAKE READY A PEOPLE PREPARED FOR THE LORD

ONCE AGAIN there first had to be divine order. This time the emphasis would not be on outward, but inward order. There in the secret place of the heart would be where the glory of the Lord was next revealed.

This ordering and transforming process began with the ministry of John the Baptist. It would be a mistake to view John as an Old Testament prophet, for the Bible describes his ministry as "the beginning of the gospel of Jesus Christ" (Mark 1:1). His preaching is found at the beginning of all four Gospels. Jesus reemphasized this by declaring, "The law and the prophets were until John" (Luke 16:16). Notice that He did not say, "The law and the prophets were until *Me.*"

John's birth was announced to his father by an angel. His ministry's thrust was summed up by these words: "And he will turn many of the children of Israel to the Lord their God . . . to make ready a people prepared for the Lord" (Luke 1:16–17).

Notice he was "to make ready a people prepared for the Lord." Just as God had anointed the artisans and craftsmen in the days of Moses to build the tabernacle, so He anointed John to prepare the temple not made with hands. By the Spirit of God, he began the process of preparation for the new temple.

Isaiah prophesied of John:

> The voice of one crying in the wilderness: "Prepare the way of the Lord . . . every valley shall be exalted and every mountain and hill brought low; The crooked places shall be made straight and the rough places smooth; The glory of the Lord shall be revealed."
>
> —ISAIAH 40:3–5

These mountains and hills were not fortresses of natural elements, but rather, the ways of man that opposed the ways of God. The towering and lofty pride of men had to be made low. The irreverence and foolishness of man would be confronted and leveled in preparation for the revelation of the glory of the Lord.

The Hebrew word for "crooked" in the above verse is *aqob.* *Strong's* defines it as "fraudulent, deceitful, polluted, or crooked." It is easy to see that crooked is not in reference to a lack of physical straightness. A more accurate translation of this word *aqob* would be "deceitful."

John was not sent to those who did not know the name of the Lord. He was sent to those in covenant with Jehovah. Israel had become religious, yet believed everything was fine. In truth God saw the Israelites as lost sheep. The thousands who faithfully attended the synagogue remained unaware of their true heart condition. They were deceived and thought their worship and service to be acceptable to God.

John exposed this deceit and tore aside the shroud of such deception. He shook the unstable foundation on which they had justified themselves as Abraham's seed. He brought to light the error in the doctrines of their elders, and exposed their formula prayers void of passion and power. He showed the futility of paying tithes while neglecting and even robbing the poor. He pointed out the emptiness of their lifeless religious habits and clearly revealed that their hardened hearts were far from God.

John came preaching a baptism of repentance (Mark 1:4). The Greek word for "baptism" is *baptisma* and is defined as "immersion." According to Webster's, *immersion* means "to plunge." So John's message was not of partial repentance but of a radical, complete change of heart.

John's bold confrontations destroyed the false security the Israelites had found in their firmly rooted deceptions. His message was a call for men to turn their hearts back to God. His divine assignment leveled the ground of the hearts that received him. The lofty mountains of pride and haughty hills of religion were made flat, preparing the people to receive the ministry of Jesus.

THE MASTER BUILDER

ONCE JOHN'S work was complete, Jesus came to prepare the temple on the level ground of humility until the building process was complete. Jesus laid the foundation and built: "For no other foundation can anyone lay than that which is laid, which is Jesus Christ" (1 Cor. 3:11).

Once again God's Word brought divine order. But this time His Word was revealed as God's Word made flesh! Jesus is the Master Builder (Heb. 3:1–4), not only by His teachings, but in the life He lived. In every way He showed forth to mankind the acceptable way of the Lord.

Those who received John's ministry were ready to receive the work of their Master Builder. Conversely, those who rejected

John were unprepared to receive the words of Jesus, for the ground of their hearts was uneven and unstable. No foundation had been laid. They were unprepared building sites incapable of supporting a sanctuary.

Jesus addressed the religious proud that resisted Him, "For John came to you in the way of righteousness, and you did not believe him; but tax collectors and harlots believed him; and when you saw it, you did not afterward relent and believe him" (Matt. 21:32). It was the sinners of the day who received the message of John and in turn opened their hearts to Jesus. "Then all the tax collectors and the sinners drew near to Him [Jesus] to hear Him" (Luke 15:1). They were not comforted in their religion and knew they needed a Savior.

THE FINAL STEP OF PREPARATION

WHEN JESUS had fulfilled all His Father had ordained for Him to do in His earthly ministry, He was sent to the cross by Caiaphas, the acting high priest, as the sacrificial Lamb. This was the final and most crucial step in the preparation of the temple of the heart of man. Jesus' sacrifice eliminated the sin nature separating man from God's presence since the fall of Adam.

We saw the offering of the sacrificial Lamb foreshadowed in the raising of the tabernacle and the dedication of the temple. When the tabernacle was raised, Aaron, as high priest, made offerings to the Lord. One of the offerings was a lamb without blemish. Once this was done, "Moses and Aaron went into the tabernacle of meeting, and came out and blessed the people. Then the glory of the Lord appeared to all the people" (Lev. 9:23). It was shortly after that Nadab and Abihu were judged and struck dead.

The sacrifice of the Lamb of God is foreshadowed in the dedication of Solomon's temple.

> Then the king and all the people offered sacrifices before the Lord. King Solomon offered a sacrifice of twenty-two thousand bulls and one hundred and twenty thousand

sheep. So the king and all the people dedicated the house of God.

—2 CHRONICLES 7:4–5

It was on this same day that the glory of the Lord was revealed in the temple.

The writer of Hebrews compares Christ's sacrifice with those offered in the tabernacle and temple by saying:

> Not with the blood of goats and calves, but with His own blood He entered the Most Holy Place once for all, having obtained eternal redemption.
>
> —HEBREWS 9:12

Jesus, the Lamb of God, hung on the cross, shedding every drop of His innocent, royal blood for us. Once this was done, the veil of the temple was torn in two from top to bottom (Luke 23:45). God moved out! God's glory would never again be revealed in a building made with hands. Soon His glory would be revealed in the temple He had always longed to dwell in.

ONE IN HEART AND PURPOSE

NOW READ what happened shortly after the resurrection of Jesus:

> When the Day of Pentecost had fully come, they were all with one accord in one place. And suddenly there came a sound from heaven, as of a rushing mighty wind, and it filled the whole house where they were sitting. Then there appeared to them divided tongues, as of fire, and one sat upon each of them.
>
> —ACTS 2:1–3

Once again the glory of the Lord is manifested. Notice, "they were all with one accord." *Divine order.* How do you get a hundred and twenty into one accord? The answer is simple. They were all dead to themselves. They had no agendas. All that mattered was that they had obeyed the words of Jesus.

We know Jesus ministered to tens of thousands in His three-and-a-half-year ministry. Multitudes followed Him. After His crucifixion and resurrection He appeared to more than five hundred followers (1 Cor. 15:6). Yet on the day of Pentecost, we find only a hundred and twenty in the house when the Spirit of God fell (Acts 1:15).

It is interesting to note that the numbers kept decreasing, not increasing. Where were the thousands after the Crucifixion? Why did He appear to only five hundred? On the day of Pentecost, where were the five hundred? It was to only one hundred and twenty that God's glory was revealed.

After His resurrection Jesus told the people not to depart from Jerusalem, but to wait for the promise of the Father (Acts 1:4). I believe that all five hundred initially waited for the promise. But as the days passed, the size of the group dwindled. Impatient, some may have decided, "We have to go on with our lives; He is gone." Others may have left to worship God in their synagogue in the traditional manner. Still others may have quoted the words of Jesus, "We must go into all the world and preach the gospel. We'd better leave now and do it!"

I believe the Lord waited until those who remained had the resolve to say within themselves, *If we rot, we are not moving, for the Master said wait.* Only those who were completely submitted to the Master could make such a commitment. No person, activity, or thing mattered as much as obedience to His words. These were the ones who trembled at His Word (Isa. 66:2). They feared God!

Those who remained had listened intently when Jesus spoke to the multitude saying:

> And whoever does not bear his cross and come after Me
> cannot be My disciple. For which of you, intending to
> build a tower, does not sit down first and count the cost,
> whether he has enough to finish it—lest, after he has laid

the foundation, and is not able to finish, all who see it begin to mock him, saying, "This man began to build and was not able to finish" . . . So likewise, whoever of you does not forsake all that he has cannot be My disciple.

—LUKE 14:27–29, 33

Jesus makes it clear that to follow Him, we must first count the cost. There is a price to following Jesus, and He makes the amount certain. The price is nothing short of our lives!

You may question, "I thought salvation was a free gift, one you cannot earn?" Yes, salvation is a gift that cannot be bought or earned. However, you cannot retain it if you do not give your entire life in exchange for it! Even a gift must be protected from being lost or stolen.

Jesus exhorts, "But he who endures to the end will be saved" (Matt. 10:22). The strength to endure is found in freely giving up your life.

A true believer, a disciple, lays down his life completely for the Master. Disciples are steadfast to the end. Converts and onlookers may desire the benefits and blessings but they lack the endurance to last to the end. Eventually they will fade away. Jesus gave the Great Commission to "go therefore and make disciples of all the nations . . . " (Matt. 28:19). He commissioned us to make disciples, not converts.

The remnant who remained on the day of Pentecost had laid aside their dreams, ambitions, goals, and agendas. This created an atmosphere where they could be of one purpose and one heart.

This is the unity God desires to bring us into today. There have been various moves for unity in our cities among some leaders and churches. We come together and seek oneness.

But we must remember that only God can truly make us one. Unless we have laid all else aside, eventually agendas that were hidden will surface. When there are hidden motives, relationships are developed on a superficial level. The outcome is shallow and nonproductive. We can have unity of purpose without obedience to the heart of our Master. Then our productivity is in vain. For, "Unless the Lord builds the house, they labor in vain who build it" (Ps. 127:1). God is still looking for those who tremble at His Word! That is where true unity is found.

THE GLORY OF THE LORD REVEALED

THOSE TOGETHER on the day of Pentecost had true unity. They were one in the purpose of their Master. Their hearts were in order. The preparation of John's ministry had coupled with the ministry of Jesus, and divine order resulted. Divine order was achieved in the hearts of men. In line with the pattern of God, after divine order came God's revealed glory. Read again what happened that day:

> And suddenly there came a sound from heaven, as of a rushing mighty wind, and it filled the whole house where they were sitting. Then there appeared to them divided tongues, as of fire, and one sat upon each of them.
> —ACTS 2:2–3

A measure of God's glory manifested on these one hundred and twenty men and women. Notice that tongues as of fire rested upon each one. Forget images you have seen in your Sunday school books—the little flames of fire floating above the heads of these disciples. Everyone present was baptized or immersed in the fire of His glorious presence (Matt. 3:11).

Of course, this was not God's full, unveiled glory, for no man has seen nor can he withstand God's full unveiled glory (1 Tim. 6:16). Yet this manifestation was strong enough to attract the attention of multitudes of devout, God-fearing Jews residing in Jerusalem from every country under heaven (Acts 2:6–7).

In answer at this point, Peter stood and preached the gospel to them. That day three thousand were saved and added to the church. It was not a scheduled service, nor had there been any advertisement. As a result:

Then fear came upon every soul, and many wonders and
signs were done through the apostles.

—ACTS 2:43

God had revealed a portion of His glory and the people were
in awe of His presence and power. He continued to work in a
mighty way. Daily there were testimonies of tremendous miracles and deliverances.

There was no denying God's mighty hand at work. Men and
women came into the kingdom in droves. Those who had previously given their lives to Jesus were refreshed by the presence of
His Spirit.

But as we have already seen, if God reveals His glory and the
people return to a lack of fear, there is certain judgment. In fact,
the greater the glory, the greater and swifter the judgment. The
next chapter will examine closely the tragic event that occurred
shortly after the revelation of God's glory.

IF YOU DESIRE THE
PRAISE OF MAN, YOU WILL FEAR
MAN. IF YOU FEAR MAN, YOU
WILL SERVE HIM——FOR YOU
WILL SERVE WHAT
YOU FEAR.

Seven

AN IRREVERENT OFFERING

He who called you is holy, you also be holy in all your conduct,
because it is written, "Be holy, for I am holy."

—1 PETER 1:15–16

TIME HAD PASSED since the day of Pentecost. The church had benefited from the presence of God and His power. Multitudes were saved, others were healed and delivered. No one lacked, for everyone shared what they had. Those with possessions sold them and brought the proceeds to the apostles for distribution to those in need.

OFFERING FROM A FOREIGNER

And Joses, who was also named Barnabas by the apostles (which is translated Son of Encouragement), a Levite of the country of Cyprus, having land, sold it, and brought the money and laid it at the apostles' feet.

—ACTS 4:36–37

Cyprus was an island abundantly blessed with natural

resources, famous for its flowers and fruits. Wine and oil were produced in abundance. There was a store of a variety of precious stones. But its chief source of wealth lay in its mines and forests. There were extensive silver, copper, and iron mines. It was a country overflowing in natural wealth. If you owned land on Cyprus, you were probably wealthy.

Picture this: A wealthy Levite named Barnabas from another land brings the total amount he received of the sale of his land, which was probably a very large sum, and places it at the apostles' disposal. Now read carefully the next verse:

> But a certain man named Ananias, with Sapphira his wife, sold a possession.
>
> —ACTS 5:1

Notice the first word of this sentence, "But." In the Bible, no new thought is introduced with the word, "but." Remember, the translators were the people who separated each book of the Bible by chapter and verse. Originally the Book of Acts was just one big letter written by a doctor named Luke.

By usage of the word "but," it is obvious that what had just happened in the fourth chapter of Acts is tied to the record of Ananias and Sapphira in the fifth chapter. In fact, I will be bold enough to say that you cannot fully understand what is about to take place without taking into account what previously happened. It would explain the reason for the word "but" at the beginning of the sentence.

Let us think this through together. A newcomer who is very wealthy joins the church and brings a very large offering from a piece of land he has sold. This man's offering causes Ananais and Sapphira to react by selling something they own. Examine the next few verses carefully:

> And he kept back part of the proceeds, his wife also being aware of it, and brought a certain part and laid it at the apostles' feet. But Peter said, "Ananias, why has Satan filled your heart to lie to the Holy Spirit and keep back part of

the price of the land for yourself? While it remained, was it not your own? And after it was sold, was it not in your own control? Why have you conceived this thing in your heart? You have not lied to men but to God."

—ACTS 5:2–4

Up to this point, Ananias and his wife most likely had the reputation in the church as being the biggest givers. They had probably received much attention from the people for their generosity. In seeing their response, I am certain that they thoroughly enjoyed this position of respect and the recognition they received for their ministry of giving.

Now they had been outdone. The attention had shifted to this new man, the Levite from Cyprus. Everyone was extolling the virtues of this generous man. The people conversed among themselves extensively about how his great gift would help so many in need. It was the talk of the church. The light of attention had been diverted from Ananias and Sapphira, creating a void they could not deal with.

They responded by immediately selling a plot of land. It was also valuable, and they received a large sum of money. It was probably their prize possession. Together they must have concluded, "This is far too much money to part with. We cannot give it all. But we want to *appear* to be giving it all. So let's give only part of it and say that it is everything we received."

Together they agreed to withhold some of the profit for themselves. But they still wanted to appear as if they had given the entire amount. Deception was their sin. It was not wrong to keep some of the proceeds from the sale. The money was theirs to do with as they wished. But it was wrong to say they had given all they'd received, when in fact that was a lie. They wanted the praises of man more than truth and integrity. Their reputations were important to them. They must have comforted themselves by saying, "What could it hurt? We're giving and meeting the needs of those less fortunate. That is the bottom line."

If you desire the praise of man, you will fear man. If you fear man, you will serve him—for you will serve what you fear. They feared man more than God. This caused them to reason away their actions and stand in the presence of God void of holy fear. If they were afraid of God, they never would have lied in His presence.

> Then Ananias, hearing these words, fell down and breathed his last. So great fear came upon all those who heard these things. And the young men arose and wrapped him up, carried him out, and buried him.
>
> —ACTS 5:5–6

This man brought an offering for the needy and wound up falling over dead! Immediate judgment occurred. Great fear came upon all those who witnessed or heard about it. Continue reading:

> Now it was about three hours later when his wife came in, not knowing what had happened. And Peter answered her, "Tell me whether you sold the land for so much?" She said, "Yes, for so much." Then Peter said to her, "How is it that you have agreed together to test the Spirit of the Lord? Look, the feet of those who have buried your husband are at the door, and they will carry you out." Then immediately she fell down at his feet and breathed her last. And the young men came in and found her dead, and carrying her out, buried her by her husband. So great fear came upon all the church and upon all who heard these things.
>
> —ACTS 5:7–11

It is quite possible that Ananias and his wife were some of the first to receive salvation through grace. They may have been the biggest givers in the church. They may have sacrificed their social standing and financial security in service to God. But sacrifices are useless when unaccompanied by hearts that love and fear God.

Notice the last verse of scripture: "So great fear came upon all the church." Recall God's warning to Aaron when his two sons had died in the presence of God while presenting their offerings without reverence.

By those who come near Me I must be regarded as holy;
and before all the people I must be glorified.

—LEVITICUS 10:3

Over the centuries God had not changed. His Word and level of holiness had not varied. His Word had not faltered since its release some two thousand years before. God was, is, and will always be the great King, and He must be reverenced as such. We cannot treat what He calls holy lightly.

The Bible doesn't say great fear came upon the *city,* but rather great fear came upon the *church.* The church was enjoying the presence of the Lord and all His benefits. When the people were filled with the Holy Spirit they acted like drunk men. I'm sure some laughed with joy and the wonder of it all as they all spoke in tongues. Why else would they have been mistaken for being drunk at nine o'clock in the morning (Acts 2:15)?

Perhaps with the passage of time the people became too familiar with the presence of God. It became common to some of them. Maybe they remembered how approachable Jesus had been and decided now that their relationship with the Holy Spirit would become similar. Although Jesus is the Son and the express image of God made flesh, we cannot forget He came as the Son of man, and mediator, because man *could not* approach the holiness of God.

Though they are one, there is a differential between God the Father, God the Son, and God the Holy Spirit. Even Jesus said men could speak against Him and it would be forgiven but not against the Holy Spirit. Jesus was letting them know ahead of time that a holy divine order was about to be restored. Before the coming of the Son, the people had been afraid or scared of God without fearing Him. Now man was restored to God, and divine order had to be reestablished.

The church wakes up to the holiness of God when Ananias and Sapphira fall dead at Peter's feet. *Maybe we should rethink some things,* some may have wondered. Others may have thought, *That easily could have been me.* Others had their concept of God jolted! *I guess I don't know Him as well as I thought I did. I would not have thought Him to bring such swift and severe judgment.* But everyone exclaimed in wonder and amazement, "He is holy and all knowing!" Great fear came upon all the church as they searched their hearts, amazed by this God of awe and wonder. So loving and yet so holy. No one remained unaffected by this startling event.

CONDUCT YOURSELVES IN THE FEAR OF GOD

PETER, WHO both walked with Jesus and witnessed this judgment, later wrote by inspiration this heartfelt admonishment:

> He who called you is holy, you also be holy in all your conduct, because it is written, "Be holy, for I am holy." And if you call on the Father, who without partiality judges according to each one's work, conduct yourselves throughout the time of your stay here in fear.
> —1 PETER 1:15–17

Notice he does not say "conduct yourselves in love." Yes, we are to walk in love, for without it we have nothing! Apart from His love, we cannot even know the Father's heart. Earlier in this very epistle, Peter comments on the love which is to burn in our hearts for the Lord, "whom having not seen you love" (1 Pet. 1:8). We are called to have a personal love relationship with our Father, but Peter is quick to add the balance of the fear of God. Our love for God is limited by a lack of holy fear. Our hearts are to bear the light and warmth of both flames.

You may wonder how this love could be limited. You can only love someone to the extent that you know them. If your image of God falls short of who He is, then you have but a surface knowledge of the One you love. True love is founded in the truth of who God really is. Do you think He reveals His heart to those who take Him lightly? *Would you?* In fact, God has chosen to hide Himself (Isa. 45:15). The psalmist refers to His place of hiding as "the secret place" (Ps. 91:1).

It is here in secret that we discover His holiness and His greatness. But only those who fear Him will find this secret refuge. For we are told:

> The secret of the Lord is with those who fear Him, and He will show them His covenant.
>
> —PSALM 25:14

Now you can more fully understand Peter's words. Paul, who did not walk with Jesus on earth but met Him on the road to Damascus, fortified this exhortation by adding the word "trembling." He says to the believers, "Work out your own salvation with fear and trembling" (Phil. 2:12). In fact, this phrase is used three times in the New Testament to describe the proper relationship between a believer and Christ.

Paul came to know Jesus by revelation of the Spirit. This is the same way we are to come to know Him. "Even though we have known Christ according to the flesh, yet now we know Him thus no longer" (2 Cor. 5:16). If we seek to access the knowledge of God, and walk with Him as we walk with natural, corruptible men, we will eventually take His presence for granted, as some did in the early church.

I'm sure Ananias and Sapphira were a part of those who were astonished and excited in the early church of Acts. All had been amazed by the abundant signs and wonders. Yet even signs and wonders will become commonplace when there is a lack of the fear of God in your hearts. The fear of God would have restrained the foolishness of this unfortunate couple. (See Psalm 34:11–13.) The fear would have revealed the holiness of God.

We must remember both of these unchangeable attributes: "God is love," and "God is a consuming fire" (1 John 4:8; Heb. 12:29). Paul refers to the fire experienced by believers when they stand before a holy God at the judgment seat. There we will give account of our works done in the body of Christ, both good and bad (2 Cor. 5:10). Paul then warns, "Knowing, therefore, the terror of the Lord, we persuade men. . . . " (2 Cor. 5:11).

Because of God's love, we can have confidence when we

approach Him. The Bible adds that we must serve and approach Him acceptably. How? With reverence and godly fear (Heb. 12:28).

Those who have been born again know God as Abba Father. But that does not negate His position as Judge of all flesh (Gal. 4:6–7; Heb. 12:23). God makes it clear: "The Lord will judge His people" (Heb. 10:30).

Consider an earthly king with sons and daughters. In the palace, he is husband and Dad. But in the throne room, he is king and must be reverenced as such even by his wife and children. Yes, there are those times when I have sensed the Father call to me from His private chamber, arms outstretched, inviting me to "come, jump on My lap, and let's embrace and talk." I love those times. They are so special. But there are times when I am praying or participating in a service when I have feared and trembled at His holy presence.

There was one such service in August 1995 at the conclusion of a week of meetings in Kuala Lumpur, Malaysia. The atmosphere had been very difficult, and that day I sensed that we had finally experienced a breakthrough. The presence of the Lord filled the building, and several people laughed as His joy flowed. This continued for ten to fifteen minutes; then there was a pause followed by another wave of God's presence. More were touched. Again, there was a lull, then another wave of God's presence washed in with a joy that permeated the sanctuary until nearly everyone was refreshed and laughing. Then there was yet another break.

It was then that I heard the Lord say, "I am coming in one last wave, but it will be different than the others." I kept silent and waited. Within minutes a very different manifestation of God's presence permeated the building. It was awesome and almost frightening. Yet I was drawn to it. The atmosphere became charged. The same people who had been laughing only moments earlier began to weep, wail, and cry. Some even screamed as though they were on fire. Yet these were not the tormented screams of demonic activity.

As I paced the platform, this thought went through my mind:

John, don't make one wrong move or say one wrong word . . . if you do, you're a dead man. I'm not certain that would have happened, but this thought relays the intensity I felt. I knew irreverence could not exist in this awesome presence. I witnessed two different responses that day—either the people were afraid and drew away from His presence, or they feared God and drew close to His awesome presence. This was definitely not one of those times when God was whispering, "Come, jump in My lap!"

We left the meeting shrouded in awe. Many felt completely transformed by the awesome presence of God. One man who was mightily touched by His presence said to me afterward, "I feel so clean inside." I agreed, for I felt purged as well. Later I found this scripture: "The fear of the Lord is clean, enduring forever" (Ps. 19:9).

THE FEAR OF THE LORD ENDURES

THE FEAR OF the Lord *does* endure forever! If Lucifer had possessed it, he would never have fallen from heaven like lightning (Isa. 14:12–15; Luke 10:18). Lucifer was the anointed cherub on the holy mountain of God and walked in the presence of the Lord (Ezek. 28:14–17). Yet Lucifer was the first one to exhibit a lack of the fear of God.

Hear me, people of God: You can have the holy anointing oil on you, like Nadab and Abihu did. You can operate in signs and wonders, cast out demons, and heal the sick in His mighty name, yet lack the fear of the Lord! Without it your end will be no different than that of Nadab and Abihu, or of Ananias and Sapphira. For it is the fear of the Lord that causes you to stand before the presence of the Lord forever!

Adam and Eve walked in the presence of the Lord. They loved and benefited from His goodness. They had never been offended by any authority. They lived in a perfect environment. Yet they disobeyed and fell, suffering great judgment. They would never have fallen if they possessed the fear of the Lord.

The fear of the Lord *does* endure forever! If Ananias and Sapphira had feared God they would not have behaved so foolishly, for, "by the fear of the Lord one departs from evil" (Prov. 16:6).

Some may question, "Doesn't my love for God keep me from sin?" Yes, but how extensive can this love be when you lack the fear of Him? When I visited Jim Bakker in prison, he shared with me how the heat of prison had caused him to experience a complete change of heart. He experienced Jesus as the Master for the first time. He shared how he had lost his family, ministry, everything he owned, and then found Jesus.

I remember his words distinctly: "John, this prison is not God's judgment on my life but His mercy. I believe if I had continued on the path I was on, I would have ended up in hell!"

Then Jim Bakker shared this warning for all of us: "John, I always loved Jesus, yet He was not my Lord, and there are millions of Americans just like me!" Jim loved the image of Jesus that had been revealed to him. His love had been immature for it lacked the fear of the Lord. Today Jim Bakker is a man who fears God. When I asked him what he would do when he got out of prison, he quickly replied, "If I go back to the way I was, I will be judged!"

NO ONE DARED JOIN THEM

WHAT HAPPENED to Ananias and Sapphira shook the church. It brought motives of the heart to the surface for inspection. Those who saw themselves in the irreverence of Ananias and Sapphira rent their hearts in repentance. Others counted the cost more seriously before joining themselves with the assembly of believers in Jerusalem. Some may have walked away in fear of God's judgment.

Fear came upon the church, but it also awed all who heard what had happened to this couple. I'm sure it was news for some time in the city. People questioned each other, "Did you hear what happened to those followers of Jesus? A couple brought an offering for the needy and fell over dead!" The Bible records:

> None of the rest dared join them, but the people esteemed them highly. And believers were increasingly added to the

Lord, multitudes of both men and women
—ACTS 5:13–14

It would seem to be a contradiction: None dared to join, yet the next verse states that believers were increasingly added. How can believers be added when no one will join? What is actually being said here? I believe that no one dared to join themselves to Jesus until they had counted the cost. There was no more "joining" for self-seeking reasons. They came to the Lord because of who He was, not because of what He could do.

It is easy to develop quickly an attitude of irreverence when we come to the Lord for what He can do for us or give to us. It is a relationship based on blessings and events. When things don't go our way—and inevitably this will happen—we're disappointed and, like spoiled children, our respect is gone. When irreverence is judged, everyone takes stock of their lives and wrong motives are purged by the light of judgment. This is an atmosphere for true hearts of repentance filled with the fear of God.

WHY THEM?

WHY DID Ananias and Sapphira die? I know people who have lied to preachers, and they haven't been judged so severely. In fact, there have been many more irreverent acts than that of Ananias and Sapphira in church history and even in the church today. No one drops dead in services any more. The whole event seems so impossible today.

The answer is found hidden in the verses immediately following this account:

> . . . they brought the sick out into the streets and laid them on beds and couches, that at least the shadow of Peter passing by might fall on some of them.
> —ACTS 5:15

Notice they laid the sick in the *streets!* Not street, but streets— just waiting for the shadow of Peter to pass by so the sick could be healed. Now I realize what I am about to say is subject to argument, but I believe that interpretation was not limited to Peter's physical shadow alone. A shadow holds no power to heal the sick. I believe it was the cloud of God. The Lord's presence was so strong on Peter that a cloud shadowed and veiled Peter's own shadow. In the same way, when Moses came down from the mountain of God, the glory of God was shining from his face so that his own image was veiled by it. Could it be that God Himself had veiled Peter in a cloud of shadow to hide His glory? In Acts 5:15, all Peter had to do was come within a shadow's range of the sick, and multitudes on the streets were healed.

We know that a very tangible presence of God's glory rested on Peter when first Ananias and then Sapphira lied to Peter and fell over dead. In essence, Ananias and Sapphira fell over dead because they were irreverent in the presence of the Lord whose glory had been revealed already. Just as with Adam, Nadab, Abihu, and the children of Israel, once again we see the pattern of order, glory, and judgment.

In the following chapters we will apply this pattern to our present-day church. As we delve deeper, we will see why the *love of God* must be coupled with the *fear of God*.

THE GREATER GOD'S
REVEALED GLORY, THE GREATER
AND SWIFTER THE JUDGMENT OF
IRREVERENCE!

Eight

DELAYED JUDGMENT

For we must all stand before Christ to be judged. We will each receive whatever we deserve for the good or evil we have done in our bodies.

—2 CORINTHIANS 5:10, NLT

A S I WRITE, we are nearing the close of two thousand years since the resurrection of our Lord Jesus. We live on the threshold of the final weeks, days, and moments before His return. Jesus said we would know the season, but not the day or hour. (See Matthew 24:32–36.)

We are living in that season.

THE FORMER AND LATTER RAIN

PROPHETIC SCRIPTURES foretold how God would reveal His glory in a mighty way at the onset of the church age and again at the close of the church age just prior to His Second Coming. James described it:

> Therefore be patient, brethren, until the coming of the Lord. See how the farmer waits for the precious fruit of the

earth, waiting patiently for it until it receives the early and latter rain.

—JAMES 5:7

Notice James refers to both an early and latter rain. In Israel the early rain fell and moistened the dry ground at the beginning of the planting season. The rain-softened ground could receive the grain, which could firmly take root. The latter rain came right before harvest and was more appreciated because it ripened and prospered the fruit.

James used physical rain as a comparison to explain the outpouring of God's glory. The early rain fell on the day of Pentecost, as Peter confirmed:

> But this is what was spoken by the prophet Joel: "And it shall come to pass in the last days," says God, "that I will pour out of My Spirit on all flesh; your sons and your daughters shall prophesy, your young men shall see visions, your old men shall dream dreams. And on My menservants and on My maidservants I will pour out My Spirit in those days; and they shall prophesy. I will show wonders in heaven above and signs in the earth beneath: blood and fire and vapor of smoke. The sun shall be turned into darkness, and the moon into blood, before the coming of the great and awesome day of the Lord."
>
> —ACTS 2:16–20

Peter used the term "pour out." The terminology for heavy rain is "downpour." Peter could have said "drop down," but he was using terms that suited the release of rainwater. Who better than Peter to describe the outpouring of God's glory experienced on the day of Pentecost? But this description is not limited to what he had just experienced, for with the same breath he described the outpouring of God's glory prior to the great and awesome day of the Lord. The great and awesome day of the Lord did not refer to the time period in which Peter lived, but to the Second Coming of Christ.

The Spirit of God did through Peter what He'd done so many times before: He linked two distinct time periods in the same prophetic message or scripture. Yes, a great outpouring of God's Spirit began on the day of Pentecost. James called it the early rain. God's glory manifested and spread wherever the Lord sent His disciples with the gospel. No known portion of the world remained unaffected.

Yet this great outpouring did not increase in momentum. It gradually waned. It diminished, as men lost their passion for His presence and glory. In place of the love and fear that once burned hot stood the cold, lifeless altar of selfish desires. Drawn away, many became busy with religious activities and doctrines that once again obscured the purpose for which God created us—to walk with Him.

A TIME OF SELFISHNESS, EVEN IN LEADERSHIP

THIS TIME OF the waxing and waning of God's presence and glory could be compared to the time period between the leadership of Moses and King David. In the days of Moses the children of Israel wandered in the wilderness for years under God's manifested glory. The irreverent were judged and met death in the desert.

But the younger generation feared the Lord and followed Him with all their hearts. They went on to possess their Promised Land under the leadership of Joshua. However, "When all that generation had been gathered to their fathers, another generation arose after them who did not know the Lord nor the work which He had done for Israel" (Judg. 2:10).

This new generation's disobedience led them back into bondage and hardship. Periodically God raised up a man or women as a judge to lead them. Through these leaders erupted spurts of revival and restoration for His people. Even though these strong leaders were raised up by God to lead, the overall condition of Israel continued to worsen. Israel responded to their judges, not to God, for we are told, "When the judge was dead, that they reverted and behaved more corruptly" (Judg. 2:19).

With each passing generation, the hearts of God's chosen people grew colder and colder until they had reached an all-time low. Such was their condition when Eli was priest and judge. After ruling Israel for forty years, his heart was dull and his sight almost completely lost.

Under Eli, acting as priests and leaders, were his two sons, Hophni and Phinehas. Their corruption exceeded their father's. This family of leaders was so offensive to God that He declared, "The iniquity of Eli's house shall not be atoned for by sacrifice or offering forever" (1 Sam. 3:14).

Such offensive leadership was the reason that the nation hit its all-time low. In times past when the nation strayed, the leaders would guide the people back to God, but these leaders pushed the people away with their persistent abuse of position and perversion of power.

Eli's sons engaged in sexual relations with the women who assembled at the door of the tabernacle. Not only were they sexually immoral, but they also used their position of leadership to coerce into immorality the women who had come to seek the Lord (1 Sam. 2:22). They abused the power of the position God had given them in order to serve His people, and instead used it as a means of fulfilling their own desires. Their actions greatly upset the Lord. Eli knew of his sons' immorality and greed, yet he did not restrain them from continual sin or remove them from their positions of leadership.

Their second violation was in the area of offerings. Again they used their God-given authority to satisfy their own greed by fattening themselves with offerings taken by manipulation and threats.

DELAYED JUDGMENT

COMPARE THE SIN of Eli's sons with the sin of Aaron's sons, Nadab and Abihu (the men who died when they brought profane fire before the Lord). It is hard to avoid questioning why Eli's sons were not judged with death just as quickly. Their sin was blatant, total disrespect for God, His people, and His offerings. Why then were they not judged the same—with immediate death at the tabernacle? Our answer is found in the following verse:

> The word of the Lord was rare in those days; there was no widespread revelation. And it came to pass at that time, while Eli was lying down in his place, and when his eyes had begun to grow so dim that he could not see, and before the lamp of God went out in the tabernacle of the Lord where the ark of God was.
>
> —1 SAMUEL 3:1–3

Note the following:

- *The word of the Lord was rare*—God was not speaking as He had with Moses. Where His Word is rare, so is His presence.
- *There was no widespread revelation*—Revelation is found in the presence of the Lord (Matt. 16:17). There was a limited knowledge of His ways due to the lack of His presence.
- *The eyes of leadership were so darkened that they could not see*—In Deuteronomy 34:7 we find, "Moses was one hundred and twenty years old when he died. His eyes were not dim nor his natural vigor diminished." Moses never lost sight, for he walked in the midst of God's glory. His body was preserved in a greater measure.
- *The lamp of God was going out*—It was going out due to a lack of oil. The glory was so far removed that His presence was only a flicker of light.

In the case of Aaron's sons, the glory had just been revealed and was strong. Fire went out from the Lord and consumed them, and they died before the Lord. The presence and glory of God were very powerful. But Eli's sons were shrouded in the darkness of almost-blind leadership and the darting shadows of a failing lamp. The lamp of God was almost out. There was only a trace of God's presence remaining. His glory had already lifted. Instant judgment only comes in the presence of His glory. Therefore, their judgment was not immediate but delayed.

GREATER GLORY—SWIFTER JUDGMENT

THIS TRUTH MUST be settled in our hearts. Though previously mentioned, it is now increasingly more evident. The greater God's revealed glory, the greater and swifter the judgment of irreverence! Whenever sin enters the presence of God's glory, there is an immediate reaction. Sin, and anyone who willfully bears it, will be obliterated. The greater the intensity of light, the less chance darkness has to remain.

Picture a large auditorium without windows or natural light. Darkness would dominate. You would not be able to see your hand in front of you. Then strike a match. There would be light but it would be limited. The greatest portion of darkness would remain unconfronted. Switch on a single sixty-watt light. The light would increase but still darkness and shadows would permeate the majority of the large room. Then imagine it was somehow possible to place a light source as powerful as the sun in this room. You guessed it; every bit of darkness would be annihilated, and light would penetrate every formerly shadowed crack and crevice.

So it is when God's glorious presence is limited or rare. Darkness is perpetual and unconfronted. Judgment is delayed. But to the degree the light of God's glory increases, there is an increase in the execution of judgment. Paul explained it in writing:

> Some men's sins are clearly evident, preceding them to judgment, but those of some men follow later.
> —1 TIMOTHY 5:24

Ananias' and Sapphira's irreverent sin was exposed by the intense light of God's glory and therefore received immediate judgment. This explains why many today whose sin exceeds theirs have escaped immediate judgment only to await delayed punishment. These are not unlike Eli's sons. They continue to sin, blindly comforted because they have failed to realize that they will yet be judged. *Nothing happened,* they think with a sigh of relief. *I must be exempt from God's judgment. He overlooks what I do.* These individuals are comforted by a false sense of grace, mistaking God's delay of judgment for the denial of it.

Those of us who are living during the latter part of the twentieth century have witnessed sin go rampant and unchecked in the church, not only among members but among leaders as well. In my last ten years of travels, rarely will three weeks go by without my hearing of a pastor, minister, elder, or some other church leader involved in sexual sin, usually with women in their church.

My heart has been pained also by the manipulation and deception surrounding the giving and taking of offerings. Not only have there been lies made about offerings as with Ananias and Sapphira, but several times I have heard of church leadership or administrators embezzling or misappropriating church funds. I've listened as two accountants who specialize in ministries from two separate states poured their hearts out to my wife and I about the greed and deceit they'd seen among ministries. One said, "If another minister comes in my office trying to find a way to get more money and evade tax laws, I am going to close up shop."

We have seen offerings motivated by greed and want rather than the sake of the people. Paul said, "Not that I seek the gift, but I seek the fruit that abounds to your account" (Phil. 4:17). Quite contrary to this, I have listened as leaders connived ways to extract the largest offering possible from God's people. I have seen the use of manipulative letters written by consulting firms, containing twisted truths to get finances. Some of these consultants even brag about how they have it down to a science, and can accurately project what the response will be. Peter warned that leadership would arise in the last days who, "In their greed . . . will make up clever lies to get hold of your money . . . and their destruction is on the way" (2 Pet. 2:3, NLT).

If this behavior had taken place in the atmosphere found in the Book of Acts, judgment would have been certain and swift. However, judgment is delayed today, for the lamp of God has grown dim. The latter outpouring of God's glory is yet to come.

Solomon lamented, "I have seen wicked people buried with honor. How strange that they were the very ones who frequented the Temple and are praised in the very city where they committed their crimes" (Eccles. 8:10, NLT)! He said these corrupt people frequently went to the temple (church) and were well thought of. It would seem they had mocked God by their deeds and had passed away with no apparent judgment. The reason—judgment was delayed.

Solomon continues, "When a crime is not punished, people feel it is safe to do wrong. But even though a person sins a hundred times and still lives a long time, I know that those who fear God will be better off" (Eccles. 8:11–13, NLT). Why will they be better off? Because judgment delayed is *not* judgment denied.

We are forewarned in the following scriptures: "The great Judge is coming. He is standing at the door!" (James 5:9, NLT).

"For we must all stand before Christ to be judged. We will each receive whatever we deserve for the good or evil we have done in our bodies" (2 Cor. 5:10, NLT).

"'The Lord will judge His people. It is a fearful thing to fall into the hands of the living God'" (Heb. 10:30–31).

These exhortations were written to believers, not sinners on the street!

Eli's sons felt safe in their sin. Perhaps their titles or work for the church had seduced them. Perhaps they judged themselves according to the standard of those around them. Whatever the reasoning, Eli's sons were deceived for they believed the *delay* of God's judgment meant the *absence* of it. This corruption of leadership only intensified the decay of Israel's deteriorating spiritual condition.

PERVERTED GRACE

PAUL HAD SOME very sobering predictions about man's

condition to describe the times we are living in today. He wrote, "In the last days there will be very difficult times. For people will love only themselves and their money. They will be boastful and proud, scoffing at God, disobedient to their parents, and ungrateful. They will consider nothing sacred. They will be unloving and unforgiving; they will slander others and have no self-control; they will be cruel and have no interest in what is good. They will betray their friends, be reckless, be puffed up with pride, and love pleasure rather than God" (2 Tim. 3:1–4, NLT).

The most somber truth is that Paul is not describing society but the church, for he continues: "They will act as if they are religious, but they will reject the power that could make them godly" (2 Tim. 3:5, NLT). They will frequently attend church, hear God's Word, talk God's Word, boast in the saving grace of the Lord, but will reject the power that could make them godly.

What is the power that could make them godly? The answer is simple: It is the very grace of God of which they boast. For the past twenty to thirty years, the grace taught and believed in many of our churches is not real grace, but a perversion of it. This is the result of overemphasizing the *goodness* of God to the neglect of the *fear* of Him.

When the doctrine of the love of God is not balanced with an understanding of the fear of God, error is the result. Likewise, when the fear of God is not balanced by the love of God, we have the same results. This is why we are exhorted to "consider the goodness and severity of God" (Rom. 11:22). It takes both—and without both, we end up unbalanced.

In numerous conversations and from many pulpits, I have heard believers and leaders excuse disobedience by marking everything off as covered by God's grace or His love. Grace *is* unmerited; and it *does* cover—but not in the manner we've been taught. It is not an *excuse* but an *empowerment*.

This lack of balance infiltrates our reasoning until we feel at complete liberty to disobey God whenever it is inconvenient or not to our advantage. Even as we sin we assure ourselves and quiet our consciences with a shrug and the thought, *God's grace will cover this, for He loves me and understands how tough life can be. He wants me happy, no matter the cost! Right?*

Granted, we do not usually verbalize this thought process, yet it exists just the same. It is evidenced by the fruit of this reasoning so accurately foretold by Paul.

Although grace covers, it is not merely a coverup. It goes far beyond that. Grace enables and empowers us to live a life of holiness and obedience to the authority of God. The writer of Hebrews exhorts, "Let us have grace, by which we may serve God acceptably with reverence and godly fear" (Heb. 12:28). The description of grace here is not that of coverup or a fluffy rug to hide everything under, but the force that empowers us to serve God acceptably with due reverence and godly fear. It is the essence of the power behind a life of obedience. It is the validation or proof of our salvation.

In rebuttal, some may argue, "But the Bible says, 'By grace you have been saved through faith, and that not of yourselves, it is the gift of God'" (Eph. 2:8–9, NAS). Yes, this is true; it is impossible in our own strength to live a life worthy of our inheritance in the kingdom of God, for all have sinned and fallen short of God's righteous standard. None of us will ever be able to stand before God and claim that our works, charitable deeds, or good lives have earned us the right to inhabit His kingdom. Every one of us has transgressed and deserves to burn in the lake of fire eternally.

God's answer for our shortcomings is the gift of salvation through His gift of grace, a gift that cannot be earned (Rom. 4:4). Many in the church understand this. Yet we have failed to emphasize the power of grace not only to redeem us, but also to grant us its ability to live our lives in a totally different manner. The Word of God declares:

> Faith by itself, if it does not have works, is dead. But someone will say, "You have faith, and I have works." Show me your faith without your works, and I will show you my faith by my works.
>
> —JAMES 2:17–18

James was not contradicting Paul. He was clarifying Paul's message by stating that the evidence a person has received God's grace is a life of obedience to the Lord. This grace not only imparts a *desire* for reverent obedience but the *ability* to follow through. A person who consistently disobeys God's Word is one in whom faith has failed or in whom faith never truly existed. James continues:

> You see then that a man is justified by works, and not by faith only.
>
> —JAMES 2:24

James prefaced this statement by using Abraham, the father of faith, as the example: "Was not Abraham our father justified by works [notice, *justified by works*] when he offered Isaac his son on the altar" (James 2:21)? Faith was evidenced by Abraham's actions. His actions or works verified that his faith was made perfect. "And the Scripture was fulfilled which says, 'Abraham believed God, and it was accounted to him for righteousness'" (James 2:23).

In our language the word *believe* has been reduced to mental acknowledgment of something's existence. Multitudes have prayed the sinner's prayer because they were moved emotionally, only to return to their original paths of disobedience. They continue living for themselves, all the while trusting in an emotional salvation that was void of the power to change them. Yes, they believe in God—but the Bible states, "You believe that there is one God. You do well. Even the demons believe—and tremble!" (James 2:19).

What good is it to acknowledge Jesus Christ when there is no change of heart and therefore no change in action?

The Scriptures portray a very different meaning for the word *believe*. It is more than the acknowledgment of the existence of Jesus; it carries with it obedience to His Word and His will. This explains Hebrews 5:9: "And having been perfected, He became the author of eternal salvation to all who obey Him." To believe is to obey, and to obey is to believe. The proof of Abraham's belief was his corresponding obedience. He offered his precious son up to God. Nothing, not even his son, meant more to Abraham than obeying God. This is true faith. It is why Abraham is honored as "the father of faith" (Rom. 4:16). Do we see this same faith and grace evident in our churches today? How have we been so deceived?

"GOD IS LIKE US"

NOT ONLY DID Eli and his sons deceive the people of Israel but they themselves were also deceived. They believed God winked at their disobedience. With seared consciences, they thought God was altogether like them. They measured Him by what they knew and saw.

Paul continued by describing those in the church of our day who lack the power to make themselves godly. "They will go on deceiving others, and they themselves will be deceived" (2 Tim. 3:13, NLT).

His prophetic insight is confirmed today. To the corrupt leaders and false believers in the church, God declares:

> Recite my laws no longer, and don't pretend that you obey me. For you refuse my discipline and treat my laws like trash. When you see a thief, you help him, and you spend your time with adulterers. Your mouths are filled with wickedness, and your tongues are full of lies. You sit around and slander a brother.
>
> —PSALM 50:16–20, NLT

God asks, "Why are you preaching My Word when you do not fear and obey Me? Why deceive others and yourselves?" He tells them:

> These things you have done, and I kept silent; You thought that I was altogether like you; But I will rebuke you, And set them in order before your eyes.
>
> —PSALM 50:21

God said, "I kept silent." Judgment was delayed, yet not denied, for the Lord assured, "I will rebuke you, and set them in order . . . " Remember, *divine order* precedes *revealed glory.* Once the glory is revealed, disorder is met with immediate judgment to assure the maintenance of divine order. God promised those whose judgment is waiting, "Know for sure there will be order, for I will bring it."

Notice it is their consciences that comfort the disobedient in their irreverent behavior. They believe God to be altogether like them. They reduce the image of the glory of God to the level of corruptible man!

People of God, hear His words of mercy! You may say, "Words of mercy? I thought you were speaking of judgment?" No, in prophetic preaching and writing, God seeks to warn us in order to keep us from His judgment. His message is therefore one of *mercy!*

GOD HAS A REMNANT

BY THE SPIRIT of God, Paul saw God's manifested glory wane until it would again reach an all-time low. The days preceding the second outpouring would see just such a spiritual climate. Both priest and people would suffer corruption. Paul prophetically lamented:

> For a time is coming when people will no longer listen to right teaching. They will follow their own desires and will look for teachers who will tell them whatever they want to hear.
>
> —2 TIMOTHY 4:3, NLT

It is sad to say, but we are living in those days. Too many pastors and ministers seem to desire attracting crowds over upholding righteousness. They are afraid to preach the truth with boldness, worried that they will jeopardize all they've worked hard to build. So they tell the people what they want to hear and sidestep confrontation.

The results are devastating. Sinners sit in our congregations unconvicted of sin and unaware of what righteousness is all about. Many of these confused individuals assume they are saved, when in fact they are not. At the same time, some ministers pursue the favor and rewards of man without considering the favor of God, while godly believers cry out, "Where is God?" Worst of all, while our society remains captive to darkness, the church is viewed with disdain. The church cannot really help society because it is infected and diseased with a lack of the fear of the Lord.

What is God's answer? It is found in the word *remnant.* Just a God found a remnant who trembled at His word to fill with His glory in the former rain, so shall He find a remnant of believers in these last days of the latter rain through which He will again reveal His glory. The size or number of this group is not important. These believers will love and obey Him no matter the expense to their personal lives. There are leaders, ministers, and believers throughout the earth today who are crying out for just such an outpouring.

WHERE WE HAVE
BEEN AND WHERE WE ARE
IS NOT WHERE WE ARE HEADED!
WE MUST RAISE OUR EYES TO
THE HORIZON AND LOOK FOR
HIS COMING GLORY!

Nine

THE COMING GLORY

*"The glory of this latter temple shall be greater than the former," says
the Lord of hosts.*

—HAGGAI 2:9

FREQUENTLY I hear ministers and believers boast that we
are in the latter rain. They talk as though the church is
currently experiencing the great outpouring of God's Spirit
foreseen by the prophets, as if Jesus could come any day and rap-
ture us away. I hear it over and over again. To those who say this
I respond, "Your vision is too small! You have settled for far less
than what God will actually do."

Often this is done out of ignorance and is most prone to
happen during a genuine move of God. As wonderful as a move
of God's Spirit in these meetings is, it still does not mean we are
experiencing the glory of the latter rain. We have confused a fresh
move of God's Spirit, which many times is accompanied by His
power, anointing, and gifts, with God's glory that is yet to come.
We fail to see God's coming glory with the eyes of our heart.

With others, such proclamations are made out of spiritual
laziness. They have grown weary of pressing on to the high

calling of God and have camped at a site far below where God has called them. Some have not camped but are aimlessly wandering alternate paths of ease. These roads bear names such as compromise, worldliness, religion, and false unity. In either case, the individuals who travel these paths have settled for the glory of man and—if left to slumber—will end up resisting God's glory when it is finally revealed.

Others have proclaimed the outpouring of God's glory out of pure hype. This is most dangerous because it is very irreverent. God spoke to my heart, "Those who settle for the *artificial* will never see the *real.*" If their irreverence continues, these people will experience judgment at the revelation of God's glory, glory intended to bring great refreshing and joy.

Some may argue, "But there is an *increase* of God's power, healing, and miracles today." This may be true, but it does not automatically indicate the latter rain. We must remember that the gifts of the Spirit can be in operation in those who are still not pleasing to the Lord. When the anointing of God comes, it does not necessarily mean that it is accompanied by the approval of God. Jesus warned that many will come to Him in the day of judgment and say they had cast out demons, prophesied, and done many wonders in His name, yet He will say to them, "Depart, you who practice lawlessness!"

We must keep in mind God's purpose for creation. He did not put Adam in the garden to have a worldwide preaching, healing, or deliverance ministry. No, Adam was placed in the garden so God could walk with him. God wanted a relationship with Adam, but the relationship was cut off due to Adam's disobedience.

We have been created for God, to coexist with His glory. But disobedience cannot exist within us if we are to please God. The accurate measurement of our true spiritual condition lies in our actual obedience to His will. There can be an anointing on our lives, yet we may still be far from God's heart. Consider the examples of Judas, Balaam, and King Saul: Each operated in the anointing, but fell short of walking in God's glory because of their selfish motives.

God does not raise His children for the purpose of performing miracles. God spoke through Balaam's donkey in the Old Testament, but that did not make this beast of burden a habitation of God's glory! For the past six millenniums God has been patiently working on a temple for Himself, formed by His obedient children who love and fear Him. Peter wrote, "You also, as living stones, are being built up a spiritual house. . . . " (1 Pet. 2:5). And Paul affirmed, "In whom you also are being built together for a dwelling place of God in the Spirit" (Eph. 2:22).

If we are honest we'll admit that we—His temple—are not yet prepared for His glory. The temple is still under construction. Divine order is being restored within the heart of man.

OUR PRESENT CONDITION

THERE IS another time period in Israel's history that parallels the present condition of the church. Remember that Israel's events and lessons are types and shadows of things to come in the church. After seventy years of Babylonian captivity, a group of Jews returned to their beloved Promised Land. Judgment was past and restoration had begun. It was time to rebuild the walls and temple.

Initially this phase of the rebuilding was met and infused with enthusiasm, dedication, and hard work. However, as the initial excitement wore thin, the people lost their motivation, and sixteen years later they had yet to finish the temple. Their personal affairs had taken precedence over the restoration of God's house. Their reverence had ebbed away in the entanglement of their own affairs. What God considered important and holy had been moved to the back burner.

To awaken the people, God raised up the prophet Haggai. He confronted the people with this question, "Is it time for you yourselves to dwell in your paneled houses, and this temple to lie in ruins?" (Hag. 1:4). The Israelites had lost their perspective because their focus had slipped from God to themselves. Whenever this happens, personal passion and desire for God always begin to wane.

Through this prophet, God explained the reason for such

dissatisfaction: "'You looked for much, but indeed it came to little; and when you brought it home, I blew it away. Why?' says the Lord of hosts. 'Because of My house that is in ruins, while every one of you runs to his own house. Therefore the heavens above you withhold the dew, and the earth withholds its fruit'" (Hag. 1:9–10). The rain had been withheld from their harvest. Whenever our pursuit is for "blessings" instead of for the Lord, He will remove or withhold so that we will cry out for Him again.

Is our dilemma today so different? We too live in an era of restoration, for the Bible tells us that Jesus will not return until the restoration of all things. (See Acts 3:21.) The Scriptures promise all that was lost will be restored before His return. God restored Israel's natural temple, yet our temple is not a natural one but the altar composed of our hearts. This holy temple will be repaired and restored to its divine order for His glory once again.

Yet in our season of restoration, we have behaved as Israel did. We have pursued the blessings and sought out comfort and ease. For most of us, our best has been given to build our own "paneled houses." We have given the majority of our time to achieve personal success so that we can enjoy comfort and security.

WHERE IS MY HONOR?

LATER GOD questioned Israel again through the last Old Testament prophet, Malachi. He lived within a century of Haggai during the same restoration period. He cried out:

> "A son honors his father, and a servant respects his master. I am your father and master, but where are the honor and respect I deserve? You have despised my name! But you ask, 'How have we ever despised your name?' You have despised my name by offering defiled sacrifices on my altar. Then you ask, 'How have we defiled the sacrifices?' You defile them by saying the altar of the Lord deserves no respect. When you give blind animals as sacrifices, isn't that wrong?

And isn't it wrong to offer animals that are crippled and diseased? Try giving gifts like that to your governor, and see how pleased he is!" says the Lord Almighty.

—MALACHI 1:6–8, NLT

God asked His people, "You call Me Lord, but where are My honor and reverence?" How was He not respected? He was given second-best while the people retained the best for themselves.

God called the people's actions disrespect and irreverence. In order to help the Israelites see their error more clearly, God challenged them to "offer what you have given Me to your governor (i.e., boss, delegated leadership, far below the level of King of the Universe)!" If the majority of us worked for our employer the way we work for God, we'd be fired before the week was out.

Let's look at the degree of honor we often give to God. We come to church ten minutes late. We sit and watch, never lifting a finger to serve, all the while criticizing the leadership and those who do serve. We keep a constant and suspicious watch over how the money is spent even though we rarely give our own tithe in its entirety. In a rush to eat, we leave before the service is dismissed. We attend only regular services and are frustrated when special meetings are called. If the weather is bad, we stay home to avoid the inconvenience. If it is exceptionally lovely, we stay home to enjoy it. If our favorite program is on TV, we will miss the service to watch it.

How long would this job-performance level last in a place of occupation?

The majority of those who do serve in churches or ministries are over-worked because only a few are willing to give their time toward carrying the tremendous workload involved in ministry. Most come only to receive or to be spectators, never to give or serve. So the poor and needy in the congregation go neglected because those with substance are too busy with their own lives. But when we get down to the bottom line, everyone is busy pursuing their own success and are most critical of the pastor if the needs of the poor are not met.

This sort of behavior is nothing else than irreverence before the Lord. Most of us today will work long, hard hours to maintain a standard of living. Yet it pains us if the service on Sunday goes a half-hour over the time we believe it should conclude. Prayer meetings are too much effort to attend, and we complain that we don't have time to feed and clothe the poor.

The truth is that everything is a strain. Many fathers will not even make time for the very families they work so hard to provide for. They push their families aside, saying defensively, "Of course I love you; can't you see I'm busy providing for you? Now, leave me alone; I'm tired and I don't have time for you right now!"

God explains their turmoil: "You are looking for much, but indeed you have little; for when you bring it home, I will blow it away. Why?" says the Lord of hosts. "Because of My house that is in ruins, while every one of you runs to his own house. Therefore the latter rain is withheld from you and the fruit of the harvest has not come" (Hag. 1:9–10, author's paraphrase).

WHERE ARE THE TRUE PREACHERS?

MALACHI AND Haggai were true prophets. Their strong prophetic words brought about change in the hearts of Israel. Israel heard these words and "obeyed the voice of the Lord their God, and the words of Haggai the prophet, as the Lord their God had sent him; and the people feared the presence of the Lord" (Hag. 1:12).

Reverence was restored. Now the focus was again upon the temple, their personal interests were secondary. When we fear God we will always place His interests and desires above our own.

We need preachers today like Haggai or Malachi, ones who will shun the popularity of the people in order to please God. We need preachers who will speak faithful words, words the people *need* to hear, as opposed to words they *want* to hear. Today, if a person writes a book on how to improve one's lifestyle or achieve success, it will sell well. We write and preach on topics that are palatable to the people. But where are those who don't consider their message's reception on earth, but only its reception in heaven?

As I travel, my time to speak is often limited by certain constraints, usually kept within an hour and a half. Normally there are two reasons behind this. First, there is the fear that if services go too long, the host church will lose evening attendance as well as membership. It is interesting that the same temperamental members can sit through two hours or more at the movies or a two-hour big sports event, but are frustrated if the sermon runs over sixty minutes.

Second, there is the strain such services place upon the children's workers. If the children's workers ministered to the children instead of entertaining them, they would experience a genuine move of God! I have held several services which lasted three hours or more, and the children had no trouble sitting through them. The reason is that the children were not being entertained, but ministered to. This is not to say that a service must be long in order to be effective. These attitudes are simply a reflection of what we value as worthy of our attention.

I notice this more frequently in very large churches. Sometimes the reason a church is large is that it caters to lukewarm converts who can be in and out in a hurry without ever being made to feel uncomfortable.

Yes, if the Holy Spirit is not present in a service, there is no reason to go more than an hour and a half. Matter of fact, even that will become a long time without the Holy Spirit's presence. I agree with that. However, the Holy Spirit will be found in services where the leadership allows Him to do and say whatever He desires!

Recently, I was with the pastor of a large church who asked me to limit the service to an hour and a half. I looked at him and with respect for his position replied: "Is this what you want? Do you want to give the Holy Spirit time restraints? If you do, you may grow but forget having a true move of God in the church."

He conceded, "All right, but please be done in two hours."

Our last service was on a Monday evening, and I preached a very strong message. About 80 percent of the people came to the front when I gave the call to repent. I noticed my time was up so I shut down the service. I have learned that God is pleased when I respect the authority He has established over a body of believers.

I flew home early the next morning. The following day the pastor called me: "John, I felt that you were supposed to pray for my staff."

I agreed and answered, "I did too, but I was out of time."

He continued, "John, when I got home my wife was in the middle of the living room floor weeping. She looked at me and said, 'We missed God. The meetings should have gone on.' We have received calls all day testifying of the lives that were changed. Believers in the area have been calling to say, 'We hear God is doing something at your church. Is there a service tonight?' I can't believe I limited your time. God has dealt with me about it."

I replied, "Pastor, I am filled with joy for I see that you have an open heart."

He then asked me back as soon as possible to conduct a week of meetings. I wish I could report that all the pastors I have encountered who have limited the Spirit of God in their churches had the same open hearts.

God lamented over this irreverence through Jeremiah:

> A horrible and shocking thing has happened in this land—
> the prophets give false prophecies, and the priests rule with
> an iron hand. And worse yet, my people like it that way!
> But what will you do when the end comes?
> —JEREMIAH 5:30–31, NLT

It's frightening, but this passage of text describes a lot of what we see today. Often the words of so-called "prophets" in the church give no real strength to the heart of God's people. They give temporary relief with the promise of blessings. But later the people are discouraged when they become disappointed with God because the word does not come true. Haggai's and Malachi's messages pointed the people back to the heart of God. Their prophetic words brought a healthy fear of the Lord back to the people, which led to obedience.

It is unfortunate that most preaching and personal prophetic words feed wrong attitudes and concepts that have infiltrated the heart of God's children. *God wants you happy. God wants you to be blessed! There is a successful lifestyle waiting for you!* Conduct a study for yourself of the personal prophecies found in the New Testament. You will find only a few, and most dealt with chains, tribulations, and death that awaited those who would bring glory to God. (See John 21:18–19; Acts 20:22–23; Acts 21:10–11.) Quite different than the personal prophecies of today!

The Lord describes a priest as one who rules with an iron hand. This happens when pastors rule by control rather than by obedience to the leading of the Spirit. It is offensive to the Holy Spirit to be told that He has only an hour and a half, from start to close, to complete His work. It displeases Him when leaders follow a rigid pattern and make decisions outside God's counsel. But what God finds most alarming is that His people *like it that way!* For many, such limitations protect their own irreverent, self-seeking lifestyles.

With the early rain came great blessing, but it brought swift judgment as well. God asks, "But what will you do when the end comes?" I believe He is warning, "If you don't change, in the day of My glory you will be judged rather than blessed."

CONSIDER THE FORMER TEMPLE

LET'S RETURN to Haggai. The fear of the Lord was restored to the hearts of Israel, their focus returned to God. Haggai then pointed out the present condition of the temple:

> Who is left among you who saw this temple in its former glory? And how do you see it now? In comparison with it, is this not in your eyes as nothing?
>
> —HAGGAI 2:3

I believe God is asking the same of us today: "How many of you remember the church in its former glory? How does it compare now? How do we—God's temple—compare?"

To answer, for comparison let's examine the glory of the church in the Book of Acts. Pentecost, the first day of the former rain, came with such strength that it captured the attention of multitudes in Jerusalem. There had been no radio, television, or newspaper announcements. No flyers were handed out. In fact, no meeting was even scheduled. Yet God so mightily manifested Himself that multitudes heard the anointed words of Peter and thousands were saved. This meeting was not held in a church, auditorium, or stadium, but rather outdoors in the streets.

A short while later Peter and John were on their way to the temple, and they saw a crippled man who had been lame from birth. Daily, he was laid there in the street to beg. Peter lifted him to his feet, and the crippled man was healed in the name of Jesus. Within minutes a crowd of thousands had again gathered. Peter preached, and five thousand men were saved. There was not even time for an "altar call," for Peter and John were arrested before they finished preaching.

In a very short time the church had grown from one hundred and twenty to over eight thousand members.

After Peter and John were released from prison they went back to the other believers. Together they prayed with such unity that the building was shaken. That's power! Now, I know preachers who may be prone to exaggerate, but the Bible doesn't! When it says the building shook, *it shook!*

Soon afterward a man and woman bring an offering and, due to irreverence, fall over dead. Immediately following that incident we read:

> They brought the sick out into the streets and laid them on beds and couches, that at least the shadow of Peter passing by might fall on some of them.
>
> —ACTS 5:15

Notice it is "streets," not "street!" Jerusalem was no small city. The glory of God was so strong that all Peter had to do was walk past these people and they were healed!

Then the persecution became so intense in Jerusalem that the believers scattered throughout the regions of Judea and Samaria. One of them, Philip, a man who waited on widows' tables, went to a city in Samaria and preached. The entire city responded, and multitudes heeded him, when they saw the great miracles he did. The effect of the Spirit of God on that city was so great that the Bible records, "There was great joy in that city" (Acts 8:8).

Philip was told by an angel of the Lord to go to the desert where he found a man of great authority from Ethiopia. He led him to Jesus and baptized him. Then the Spirit of the Lord caught Philip away so that he disappeared right before the man's eyes. He was translated from the desert to a town named Azotus.

Soon afterward we find Peter going to a city named Lydda. There he found a man named Aeneas who had been paralyzed for eight years. Peter spoke to him in the name of Jesus, and this crippled man was immediately healed.

The Bible says, "So all who dwelt at Lydda and Sharon saw him and turned to the Lord" (Acts 9:35). Two entire cities wound up getting saved!

Later we see God working mightily among the gentiles. Everywhere the believers went, entire cities were affected. Believers were described as "these who have turned the world upside down have come here too" (Acts 17:6).

So powerful was His glory that the Bible records, "And this continued for two years, so that all who dwelt in Asia heard the word of the Lord Jesus, both Jews and Greeks" (Acts 19:10). Wow! It does not say, "All of Asia heard the word." That would be easier to swallow, for that would mean every city was affected, but would not necessarily mean every person.

Rather it says, "All who dwelt in Asia heard the word of the Lord!" That tells us every person who dwelt in Asia heard the Word of God in only two years. Asia is not a town, city, or even a country. It is a region!

All this was done without satellites, Internet, televisions, radios, cars, bicycles, audiotapes, books, or videos. Yet the Bible says *every* person heard the gospel as it was proclaimed by these early Christians.

SEVEN TIMES GREATER

ARE YOU NOW glimpsing how glorious the Acts church was during the former rain of God's Spirit? Now let's again address God's question: "How does today's church compare with the Book of Acts?" Are we not as nothing? If we were honest, we would answer *yes* to this question. There is no way to compare today's church to the glorious church of Acts. We may have more *resources,* but it seems that we have less of the *source.* I am not against books, tapes, television, computers, and satellite technology. These are all resources, but if they are not breathed upon by the Source, they will fall short. *God is the Source for all our resources.*

Does God ask this question to condemn us? Absolutely not! He is merely challenging us to increase our vision. If we think we have arrived at our destination, we will have no desire to go further. Our passion and sense for adventure will be lost. Proverbs 29:18 tells us, "Where there is no revelation (prophetic vision), the people cast off restraint."

With this revelation of our need, He makes a way for His prophetic vision.

Read God's Word and see His vision:

> "The glory of this latter temple shall be greater than the former," says the Lord of hosts.
>
> —HAGGAI 2:9

Wow! Can you envision that? God says His revealed glory will *exceed* that displayed in the Book of Acts! Do you see how short of God's vision we still are?

In fact, the Lord stunned me by speaking to me in prayer a few years ago: "John, the magnitude of My revealed glory in the coming days shall be seven times greater than what the people experienced in the Book of Acts!"

I immediately cried out, "Lord, I don't know that I can believe or comprehend that! I need to see what You have just spoken in Your Word to confirm that this is You speaking to me."

I have done this often, and the Lord has never chastened me for it. Scripture says, "By the mouth of two or three witnesses every word shall be established" (2 Cor. 13:1). The Spirit of God does not contradict His written, established Word.

The Lord immediately responded, rapidly dropping scriptures into my heart—not just two or three but several.

First He asked, "John, did I not say in my Word that when the thief is caught, he must restore sevenfold (Prov. 6:31)? The thief has stolen from the church, but My Word says that heaven must receive Jesus until the times of restoration of *all* things! That restoration will be sevenfold!"

He continued, "John, did not I say in My Word that I would cause the enemies that rose against my people to be defeated? 'They shall come out against you one way and flee before you seven ways'" (Deut. 28:7).

Then, using a verse from Ecclesiastes, He asked, "John, did not I say in my Word that 'The end of a thing is better than its beginning' (Eccles. 7:8)? The end of the church age shall be better than the beginning."

Yet one more time He spoke, asking, "John, did not I save the best wine for last at the wedding of Canaan" (John 2:1–11)? Wine speaks of His tangible presence in Scripture.

Later He showed me the scripture verse that cemented it for me in my heart. Isaiah, chapter 30, tells how God's people would seek to strengthen themselves in the strength of Egypt (the world's system). They would take strength in the idols pursued by the world. Then God would have to bring the people through adversity and affliction for purification. In this process, they would put away their idols and turn their hearts completely back to God. Once this happened God said:

> Then He will give the rain for your seed . . .
>
> —Isaiah 30:23

Isaiah is not speaking of natural rain but rather the rain of God's Spirit as described by Joel, Peter, and James. Look at what Isaiah goes on to say:

> The [light of the] sun will be seven times brighter—like the
> light of seven days! So it will be when the Lord begins to
> heal his people and cure the wounds he gave them.
> —ISAIAH 30:26, NLT

The natural sun does not shine seven times brighter when it is raining. No, God is describing the glory of His Son whom the Scriptures calls "the Sun of Righteousness" (Mal. 4:2). His glory will be seven times greater in the days just before His Second Coming.

The latter rain of God's glory will not only bring refreshing to God's people but also to those around them. I have gone to great meetings where God was moving and where there were thousands in attendance each night. Though well-attended by the saints, backsliders, and sinners, these meetings often did not even put a dent in the surrounding city. As I drove to the services, I wondered when the entire city would be affected. As wonderful as our meetings are, I still watch for the latter rain.

The latter rain is different than past revivals. These revivals affected a city or a region here or there, such as Azusa and Wales. They also affected the nations, but you had to go there to be a part of it. But in the Book of Acts His glory manifested everywhere His disciples went. The glory of God was poured out all over the known world. The latter rain will be poured out all over the earth in a much greater measure!

It is with excitement that I declare: Where we have been and where we are now *is not where we are headed!* We must raise our eyes to the horizon and look for His coming glory!

PREPARE THE WAY
OF THE LORD BY MAKING
HIS PEOPLE READY FOR
HIS GLORY!

Ten

THE RESTORATION
OF HIS GLORY

But truly, as I [the Lord] live, all the earth shall be filled with the glory of the Lord.

—NUMBERS 14:21

W E ARE RAPIDLY approaching the latter rain of God's glory. There will be a major difference between today's church and the church prior to Pentecost. In the Book of Acts God poured out His Spirit suddenly and dramatically, then years later it began to wane. I believe Scripture reveals that the latter rain will not be a sudden outpouring but a rapid restoration. The first was sudden, the latter rapidly restored.

In explanation, let's return to the timespan between Moses and King David. Moses built the tabernacle, which represented divine order, then the glory of the Lord was revealed in a powerful and dramatic way. It was sudden and awesome. No sooner had Moses completed the work than the tabernacle was engulfed in a thick cloud of the glory of God.

This glory eventually waned due to sin and indifference toward the Lord. This gradual waxing and waning continued until Israel had reached an all-time low under Eli's leadership. The lamp of God was close to going out, and His glory had departed.

The day Eli and his sons died, the ark of God was captured by the Philistines. They brought the ark to the city of Ashdod where their god Dagon was located. But the hand of the Lord was against Dagon. The statue of their god fell, its head and hands broken off before the ark of God. The Philistines moved the ark to five cities. Wherever they brought the ark, the Philistines were plagued with tumors and death. The devastation was so immense that the agony of the cries of the fifth city reached up to heaven. (See 1 Samuel 5.)

After seven months, the Philistine rulers gathered together with their priests and diviners to decide how to send the ark back to Israel. They wanted to honor the God of Israel with a guilt-offering of five gold rats and tumors, representing their five cities and their rulers. They prayed God would lift His hand of chastening from them. After placing these golden articles in a chest, they placed the chest alongside the ark on a new cart drawn by two cows that had just borne calves. The calves of these cows were put in a pen. The Philistines reasoned, *If the cows pull this cart into the territory away from the lowing of their young, then we will know it is God who has struck us.* The cows pulled the ark straight into Israel's territory, where the ark remained undisturbed in the house of Abinadab in the city of Kirjath Jearim for twenty years. It is interesting to note that Israel's first king, Saul, never sought to restore the ark of God to Israel.

THE RESTORATION OF GOD'S GLORY TO ISRAEL

AFTER THE REIGN of Saul, King David sat on the throne. His heart sought after God and longed for the restoration of His glory to Israel. But this glory was not manifested the same way as with Moses. It was not sudden and powerful, but a restoration process.

This restoration process began years earlier with the prophet Samuel. God commissioned him to prepare the way by

116

calling the people back to the heart of God. His message was the heartbeat of all true prophets.

> Then Samuel spoke to all the house of Israel, saying, "If you return to the Lord with all your hearts, then put away the foreign gods . . . and prepare your hearts for the Lord, and serve Him only; and He will deliver you."
>
> —1 SAMUEL 7:3

HONOR THAT INSULTED GOD

ONCE DAVID became king, he took Jerusalem by defeating the Philistines. Then he sought to restore the ark to its rightful place. "Then David consulted with the captains of thousands and hundreds, and with every leader" (1 Chron. 13:1). They discussed bringing all Israel together for this event. "Then all the assembly said that they would do so, for the thing was right in the eyes of all the people" (v. 4).

Read carefully what they did next:

> So they set the ark of God on a new cart, and brought it out of the house of Abinadab.
>
> —2 SAMUEL 6:3

Where did the Israelites get the idea to bring the ark back to Jerusalem on a "new cart"? Isn't this the exact way the Philistines had sent it back to Israel?

They brought the ark out of Abinadab's house with two men, Ahio and Uzzah, driving the cart. "Then David and all the house of Israel played music before the Lord on all kinds of instruments" (2 Sam. 6:5). First Chronicles 13:8 tells us they did this with all their might! Yet look what happened:

> And when they came to Nachon's threshing floor, Uzzah put out his hand to the ark of God and took hold of it, for the oxen stumbled. Then the anger of the Lord was aroused

against Uzzah, and God struck him there for his error; and he died there by the ark of God.

—2 SAMUEL 6:6–7

The New King James Bible has a reference mark by the word *error.* I traced it to my center column and found the word, *irreverence.* Another translation could read, "God struck him there for his irreverence!"

Amazing! Just a generation earlier, two men were committing adultery at the door of the tabernacle where the ark resided. Their irreverence was blatant and far exceeded this man's who merely put his hand forth to stabilize the ark. The immoral priests were not immediately judged for their behavior, yet this man Uzzah was. Why? In the case of the sons of Eli, the glory had departed. With Uzzah, the glory of God was returning. The stronger God's manifested glory, the swifter and more severe His judgment for irreverence.

AFRAID OF GOD

And David became angry because of the Lord's outbreak against Uzzah. . . . David was afraid of the Lord that day, and he said, "How can the ark of the Lord come to me?"

—2 SAMUEL 6:8–9

David, his leaders, and the people of Israel did not lack passion. There had been a great amount of preparation to restore the ark to Israel. Once the ark was repossessed by Israel, the people played music with all their might. They believed they were honoring God by bringing the ark on a new cart. David hand-picked the two men who would drive the cart. So you can understand David's shock when God struck dead one of his choice men.

His shock soon turned to anger. David may have questioned, *Why has God done this? Why has He not only been unappreciative of our zeal, but rejected it with such judgment?* David must have thought, *I have done all I knew to do to honor God and my best has been judged unacceptable!* After much thought, his anger turned to fear. He became afraid of God. (This is not the same as fearing God. Those who are afraid draw back from Him, but those who fear Him draw toward Him. We will see this later in the book). David must have wondered, *If my best was judged as unacceptable, how can the ark of the Lord come to me?*

Anytime I have experienced frustration or anger with the Lord, I have quickly affirmed to myself that it is due to my own lack of knowledge or understanding, for God's ways are perfect. I have personally learned that one may have tremendous zeal yet lack knowledge. Zeal and passion not tempered by wisdom and knowledge always lead to trouble. In addition to this, I've learned that it is my responsibility to search out the knowledge of God (Prov. 2:1–5).

NEGLECTED RESPONSIBILITY

DAVID WAS angry with the Lord, yet the judgment had come due to a lack of understanding on the part of David and his leaders. Moses said:

> These are the statutes and judgments which the Lord your God has commanded to teach you, that you may observe them in the land which you are crossing over to possess, that you may fear the Lord your God.
> —DEUTERONOMY 6:1–2

Moses gave a clear directive: To fear God we must both know and obey His ways above all else. Not only was this command issued to the children of Israel, but God gave specific commands to the king as well.

> Also it shall be, when he sits on the throne of his kingdom, that he shall write for himself a copy of this law in a book, from the one before the priests, the Levites. And it shall be with him, and he shall read it all the days of his life, that he may learn to fear the Lord his God. . . .
> —DEUTERONOMY 17:18–19

The king was to read the Word of God every day. Why? God's wisdom and honor were to be established in his heart so that he would esteem God's ways above man's ideas. The error of David and his leaders could have been avoided.

David and his men came together to discuss how they *thought* the ark should be brought back. There is no mention of their consulting God's written Word that had been passed down from Moses. If David and the priests had read the counsel of God's Word, they would have realized that the only ones who could carry the ark of God were the Levites, not by way of a cart but suspended by poles and carried on their shoulders (Exod. 25:14; Num. 4:15; 7:9). This lack of knowledge caused the Israelites to mimic the gentile, or world's, way of carrying the presence of the Lord. The Philistines were ignorant when they sent the ark back by cart, but Israel had been entrusted with the oracles of God; therefore, they were accountable.

Their negligence in seeking God's counsel through His Word resulted in the image of the glory of God being reduced yet again to the perception of corruptible man. This is why the Israelites honored God by the same method as those who had no knowledge of God. They copied man instead of receiving their inspiration from God. They were zealous, but God still viewed their methods as irreverent.

WHAT IS THE SOURCE OF OUR INSPIRATION?

WE ARE MAKING the same error today. Often our ministry ideas are forged by a gathering of men. There, we draw from the wells of our own limited wisdom, pooling our counsel, which has been unconsciously influenced by cultural trends. These trends are right in front of us, and easier to access than waiting on God for a revelation of His will. Though many new and fresh ideas are appearing, do we always know where our inspiration is coming from? We have substituted the knowledge of God for the motivational techniques gleaned from unregenerate man.

As noted in the Scriptures, music plays a significant, key role in cultivating an atmosphere for the presence of the Lord. It has the ability to open and prepare a person's heart. Consider the contemporary Christian music that is so popular today—it often gets its inspiration from the demonic music of the world. If the world has hard rock, we can too! If it has rap, we'll copy it. If the world has a certain dance, we'll imitate it. If the world has MTV (Music Television) we can too! Of course, we change the words—but the beat and presentation are the same. The list goes on. In each case, we try to copy the world and even make ours better. How far will this go? If you want to predict the new music ministry trend, don't pray—just turn on MTV and watch or listen to what the world is doing. So who is leading whom? If we are honest, we will bemoan the fact that demonized men have become our prophets. How have we been so deceived?

Some argue, "But we are using music the way they hear it. In order to reach the lost, we package music in a way that sinners can receive." That may be true in a few cases (very few, in fact), but I have found that the majority of young people who listen to this music are already in the church. The heartbreaking fact is that many times these are the same young adults who yawn or talk with one another during times of true worship! Because their flesh is so overstimulated by the world, these hip youth tend to despise the very thing they need the most.

It is heartbreaking, but many contemporary Christian radio stations communicate with their listeners the same way secular stations do, gathering their ideas from the secular stations that mock God. Yet some would argue, "We are giving Christians an alternative." What kind of disciples are developed by these practices?

People like to be entertained. The average American watches forty-five hours of TV a week. Churches have done the same thing to attract people the way the world does. In the church, we have learned how to attract people by appealing to their tendency to want to be entertained. Out of this practice has come what many call "seeker-friendly" or "seeker-sensitive" churches. Having preached in some of these churches, I have found that often what is "seeker-sensitive" is "God in-sensitive." These churches may draw large crowds, but is it worth the expense of offending God?

I have spoken at churches that spend thousands of dollars annually to entertain their people. Their youth are entertained by pinball, air hockey, foozball, and even Nintendo games. Then the church leaders wonder why there is no move of God in the youth department and are puzzled by the number of teenage pregnancies. The attendance numbers are up, but where is the fruit of the Spirit being manifested in these young lives?

This cultural inspiration is not limited to leadership, but has affected many believers as well. Let's look at one example. Our society respects authority only when they agree with it. There are bumper stickers that proclaim, "Question Authority!" This is not isolated to the world, but many churches as well have adopted this mindset. They respect and obey authority only if they agree with it. You would almost think that God's kingdom had changed into a democracy! It is alarming that this attitude extends beyond delegated authority, for the people honor God with the same indifference. If they like what He is doing in their lives, they will praise Him; if not, they complain.

The list is almost endless. The point is, much of the way we minister to the Lord is inspired by the world. What will we do in the end? What will become of our ways?

PURSUE THE KNOWLEDGE OF GOD

THERE ARE many who cry out for God to restore His glory. They are praying for the latter rain (Zech. 10:1). They are submitting to God's purification process and not complaining when they walk through trials. They do not murmur in the wilderness that they are walking through spiritually. Soon they will rejoice, for God will not withhold His glory from those who hunger for Him.

These people are a contrast to those who pursue comfort and success. Others are caught in the middle—they pursue God's presence, yet as David, theirs is a zeal not according to knowledge. They pursue God in their own way . . . by their own wisdom. They have yet to realize the glory and holiness of the One they desire.

We must not ignore the Scriptures that bring correction, instruction, and adjustments, and that lead to holiness. Hear the words of Hosea:

> Come, and let us return to the Lord; for He has torn, but He will heal us; He has stricken, but He will bind us up. After two days He will revive us; on the third day He will raise us up, that we may live in His sight.
> —HOSEA 6:1–2

This passage is a prophetic scripture describing God's refinement of His church in preparation for His glory. He has torn but He will heal. A day with the Lord is a thousand of our years (2 Pet. 3:8). It has been two full days (two thousand years) since the resurrection of the Lord. We are on the verge of God's reviving and restoring His glory to His temple. The third day speaks of the thousand-year millennial reign of Christ when He will live and reign in our sight. Hosea gives further instruction about how to live and what to pursue as we prepare for His glory.

> Let us know, let us pursue the knowledge of the Lord. His going forth is established as the morning; He will come to us like the rain, like the latter and former rain to the earth.
> —HOSEA 6:3

Hosea assures us that His glorious coming is as certain as the sunrise in the morning. There is an appointed time, whether or not we are ready. Our pursuit is to be the knowledge of the Lord. David and his men hungered for the presence of the Lord yet lacked the knowledge of God. Such knowledge could have prevented Uzzah's instantaneous death. Today is no different. We are admonished:

> My son, if you receive my words, and treasure my commands within you, So that you incline your ear to wisdom, and apply your heart to understanding; Yes, if you cry out for discernment, and lift up your voice for understanding,

> If you seek her as silver, and search for her as for hidden
> treasures; Then you will understand the fear of the Lord,
> and find the knowledge of God.
>
> —PROVERBS 2:1–5

The way to life is made clear. If someone told you there were
ten million dollars hidden somewhere in your home, you would
search for it non-stop until you found the hidden fortune. If
need be, you would pull up carpets, rip open dry wall, and even
tear the house down to the foundation in order to find that
much money. How much more important are the words of life!

When we get our inspiration from the world, we are drawing
on the wisdom of men and diviners. The reverence for God is
only taught by the commandment or directive of men. Without
the pursuit of the knowledge of God, again and again we will
find ourselves in the situation of Uzzah—filled with good
intentions yet offensive to His glory.

With the increase of God's glory in the latter days there will be
new accounts of things occurring similar to that which happened to Ananias and Sapphira. This is neither the desire of God
nor the purpose for the restoration of His glory. Such judgment
is simply the product of not properly respecting and honoring
the greatness of His glory. To the degree of glory revealed, to that
same degree judgment will be executed whenever the glory of
God is met with irreverence and disrespect.

ESTABLISHED HEARTS

LOOKING again at the Book of James, we find the same
warning:

> Therefore be patient, brethren, until the coming of the
> Lord. See how the farmer waits for the precious fruit of the
> earth, waiting patiently for it until it receives the early and
> latter rain. You also be patient. Establish your hearts, for
> the coming of the Lord is at hand.
>
> —JAMES 5:7–8

Notice James tells us to be patient. The Greek word actually means "to endure and not lose heart." Then James says, "Establish your hearts." In other words, "put your hearts in divine order and maintain that state." If not, we could find ourselves on the judgment side of His glory. Both Paul and Peter instruct us how to establish our hearts:

> As you have therefore received Christ Jesus the Lord, so walk in Him, rooted and built up in Him and established in the faith, as you have been taught, abounding in it with thanksgiving.
>
> —COLOSSIANS 2:6–7

When submission to the lordship of Jesus establishes us, then we are able to hold fast to what we've been taught in the Scriptures by the Spirit. Peter reaffirms this with:

> For this reason I will not be negligent to remind you always of these things, though you know and are established in the present truth.
>
> —2 PETER 1:12

Peter says, " . . . remind you always." He knew the importance of being established in present truth. Peter knew by personal experience how easy it was to sway from truth. As the disciple who received the revelation of who Jesus was, only to deny knowing the Messiah within a few short months of that incredible revelation, Peter knew what it was to drift away from the truth.

It is not enough only to pursue the knowledge of God. To continue in it, we must live it. Too often we live off what God did in the past and drift from experiencing Him in the present. We still quote scriptures and talk a good talk, but we lack a hunger for His ways.

We must return to the teachable nature of our first love. When we first met Him, we would read our Bibles and listen to messages with great anticipation, anxious that our Lord, the object of our love, might be revealed in greater dimensions. But all too soon, we began to slip into this type of attitude: "Let's see what this minister has." The hidden motive of our attitude was to dismiss the truth of such preaching, justifying our apathy with, "I already know that," or "I have heard it all before!" Another symptom of this attitude is listening or reading in order to glean what we want, instead of experiencing God's ways and looking for a deeper revelation of His heart. We are warned:

> Therefore we must give the more earnest heed to the things
> we have heard, lest we drift away.
>
> —HEBREWS 2:1

Many are drifting away right in our churches because they are not anchored or established in the knowledge of God. They have lost their desire to pursue the knowledge of God. The apostles and the prophets foresaw this drifting and diligently warned us to remain steadfast that we may have joy in the end.

It is fearful to consider what will happen when hearts are not in order. Many will miss the blessing of God's glory while others will fall into judgment!

THE TABERNACLE OF DAVID RESTORED

WHEN DAVID saw what happened to Uzzah, he returned to Jerusalem and diligently sought the knowledge of God. Three months later he made a proclamation:

> Then David said, "No one may carry the ark of God but
> the Levites, for the Lord has chosen them to carry the ark
> of God and to minister before Him forever."
>
> —1 CHRONICLES 15:2

This time there was no gathering of men for discussion. Once David discovered God's counsel on the matter, he boldly set it in motion. He summoned Israel and separated the descendants of Aaron and the Levites. He said to these priests:

> You are the heads of the fathers' houses of the Levites; sanctify yourselves, you and your brethren, that you may bring up the ark of the Lord God of Israel to the place I have prepared for it. For because you did not do it the first time, the Lord our God broke out against us, because we did not consult Him about the proper order.
>
> —1 CHRONICLES 15:12–13

The proper order for these priests called for them to be sanctified, and dictated the external and natural structure for bearing the ark—the presence of God. This time the ark was brought to Jerusalem into the tabernacle David had prepared, and once again God's glory was restored to Israel. Our proper order for bearing His presence is found in the recesses of the heart. It is within the heart we must prepare, for God is about to reveal His glory on earth like it has never been seen before. He declares:

> But truly, as I live, all the earth shall be filled with the glory of the Lord.
>
> —NUMBERS 14:21

When God made this statement He was grieved by the fact that His people would not believe or obey Him. The implication is that there will come a time in the future when His people will fear Him and therefore unconditionally obey Him. These believers would manifest His glory, for they would be the temple of His glory. Later God spoke through the prophet Isaiah:

> Arise, shine; for your light has come! And the glory of the Lord is risen upon you. For behold, the darkness shall cover the earth, and deep darkness the people; but the Lord will arise over you, and His glory will be seen upon you. The Gentiles shall come to your light, and kings to the brightness of your rising.
>
> —ISAIAH 60:1–3

Notice Isaiah says, "The glory of the Lord has risen upon

you." Yet we have also heard the glory described as latter rain. God spoke to me in prayer and compared the release of His latter rain to the flood of Noah. The Bible said, " . . . all the fountains of the great deep were broken up, and the windows of heaven were opened" (Gen. 7:11). His restored glory will arise on those who have prepared their hearts for Him, and it will fall upon the nations of the world. No city will be unaffected by the latter rain of His Spirit.

God says His glory will be restored to His people, and even unbelievers will be drawn to His light. Amos says:

> On that day I will raise up the tabernacle of David, which has fallen down, and repair its damages; I will raise up its ruins, and rebuild it as in the days of old.
>
> —AMOS 9:11

God's glory will be restored to the church and will exceed the glory as it was in the days of David. James quoted this scripture to the leaders of the church and applied it to the last days by saying:

> Simon has declared how God at the first visited the Gentiles to take out of them a people for His name. And with this the words of the prophets agree, just as it is written: "After this I will return and will rebuild the tabernacle of David, which has fallen down; I will rebuild its ruins, and I will set it up; So that the rest of mankind may seek the Lord, even all the Gentiles who are called by My name," says the Lord who does all these things. Known to God from eternity are all His works.
>
> —ACTS 15:14–18

By the Spirit, James saw this great harvest of believers coming into the kingdom with the restoration of His glory. He speaks prophetically, but he did not complete Amos's message, for that specifically applied to our time. Let's see the completion of Amos's message:

"Behold, the days are coming," says the Lord, "When the plowman shall overtake the reaper, and the treader of grapes him who sows seed; the mountains shall drip with sweet wine, and all the hills shall flow with it."

—AMOS 9:13

God says the harvest will be so abundant, the reaper so loaded with work that he will not be able to complete the work before the plowman comes to prepare the fields for a new season. The New Living Translation says it like this:

"The time will come," says the Lord, "when the grain and grapes will grow faster than they can be harvested."

—AMOS 9:13, NLT

Simply put, God is describing a harvest so abundant that it will be overwhelming. Glory to God! Watch for this day for it is rapidly approaching. The time is short. Do not resist His purifying work and neglect the knowledge of the Lord.

As I have written this book, I have been so aware of its importance and timing. It is a cry of the Spirit sounded out to the church. Its message—"Prepare the way of the Lord by making His people ready for His glory!" As God restores His glory, let us be wise and learn from David and his men. These events were recorded for more than historical purposes. We are told, "For whatever things were written before were written for our learning" (Rom. 15:4).

Now that we've laid the foundation for understanding the times, it is time to pursue the importance of learning to walk in the fear of the Lord.

A PERSON WHO FEARS
GOD TREMBLES AT HIS WORD
AND IN HIS PRESENCE.

Eleven

THE ABILITY TO SEE

Oh, that they had such a heart in them that they would fear Me and always keep all My commandments, that it might be well with them and with their children forever!

—DEUTERONOMY 5:29

WE FREQUENTLY hear messages derived from Paul's first letter to the church at Corinth. This book of the Bible is referenced often, especially in Spirit-filled circles. The Corinthian church was established approximately A.D. 51 (many years after the day of Pentecost), and was very open to—and therefore greatly benefited by—spiritual gifts. The anointing of the Holy Spirit was strong within its membership, not unlike several of our churches today.

Paul's second epistle to the church body at Corinth is not referenced as frequently as the first. This letter contains a greater emphasis on divine order, the fear of the Lord, and the subsequent restoration of His glory. If read in context, this letter holds a strong and exciting message for today's believers. As we examine a portion of it, keep in mind that 2 Corinthians was written to people who were no strangers to the anointing and frequently operated in spiritual gifts.

THE GLORY OF THE OLD COVENANT VS. THE NEW

IN BOTH of his letters to the Corinthians, Paul referred often to the flight of the children of Israel from Egypt and to the revelation of God's glory to them in the desert. Their experience pertains to us as well, for all that happened to the Israelites in a natural sense were types and shadows of what we would experience in the realm of the Spirit. Paul emphasizes this:

> All these events happened to them as examples for us. They were written down to warn us, who live at the time when this age is drawing to a close.
>
> —1 CORINTHIANS 10:11, NLT

Paul's first letter dealt with many fundamental elements of divine order of the heart for God's people. His second letter went deeper still. He moved on to discuss God's desire to reveal His glory and dwell in the hearts of His people. Paul began by comparing God's glory in the wilderness with His glory as revealed under the New Covenant.

In contrast, he writes:

> That old system of law etched in stone led to death, yet it began with such glory that the people of Israel could not bear to look at Moses' face. For his face shone with the glory of God, even though the brightness was already fading away. Shouldn't we expect far greater glory when the Holy Spirit is giving life?
>
> —2 CORINTHIANS 3:7–8, NLT

On the mountain Moses beheld the form of the Lord and talked with Him as a man does with his friend. When he came down from the mountain, Moses covered his face because the brilliance of it frightened the people. Moses' countenance reflected that he had been in the presence of—the glory of—God.

In the New Covenant, God's plan is not for us to *reflect* His glory, but for His glory *to be seen in us!* It is one thing to reflect something but quite another to abide in and emit it! That is God's ultimate goal! This is why Paul could say:

> In fact, that first glory was not glorious at all compared with the overwhelming glory of the new covenant.
> —2 CORINTHIANS 3:10, NLT

Even though the glory of the Old Covenant did not compare with the glory of the New, the Old was still so awesome that Paul reiterates, "Israel could not look steadily at the end of what was passing away" (v. 13). But then Paul is quick to lament:

> But their minds were blinded.
> —2 CORINTHIANS 3:14

How tragic that they could not see the very thing they needed so desperately. Paul warns us so that we might not find ourselves blind and in the same dilemma.

So we must ask, "How were their minds blinded?" The answer holds knowledge and wisdom we lack desperately. That which we lack is necessary in order for us to walk in God's glory! To obtain our answer, we must return to the time frame Paul discussed.

THE FEAR OF GOD VS. BEING AFRAID OF GOD

ISRAEL HAD JUST left Egypt and was led by Moses to Mount Sinai, where God would reveal His glory.

> Then the Lord said to Moses, "Go to the people and conse-crate them today and tomorrow, and let them wash their clothes. And let them be ready for the third day. For on the third day the Lord will come down upon Mount Sinai in the sight of all the people."
> —EXODUS 19:10–11

This message was prophetic, for it speaks of our day as well.

Before God manifested His glory, the people were to sanctify themselves. This included washing their clothes. Remember that a day with the Lord is as a thousand of our years. It is now almost two thousand years (two days) since the resurrection of the Lord Jesus Christ. God said that for those two thousand years (two days), His church was to consecrate, or set ourselves apart, from the world in preparation for His glory. Our garments were to be cleansed of the filth of the world (2 Cor. 6:16; 7:1). We were to become His bride without spot. After the two thousand years, He will again manifest His glory.

Now read the account of what happened on the morning of the third day:

> Then it came to pass on the third day, in the morning, that there were thunderings and lightnings, and a thick cloud on the mountain; and the sound of the trumpet was very loud, so that all the people who were in the camp trembled. And Moses brought the people out of the camp to meet with God, and they stood at the foot of the mountain. Now Mount Sinai was completely in smoke, because the Lord descended upon it in fire. Its smoke ascended like the smoke of a furnace, and the whole mountain quaked greatly.
> —EXODUS 19:16–18

God manifested Himself not only by sight but also by voice and sound. When Moses spoke, God answered Him in the hearing of all. Often today God is referred to as our friend in a loose sense of His almost being a buddy. If we could but glimpse what Moses and the children of Israel saw, we might have a significant change of view. He is the Lord, and He has not changed! Read carefully the reaction of the people when God came:

> Now all the people witnessed the thunderings, the lightning flashes, the sound of the trumpet, and the mountain smoking; and when the people saw it, they trembled and stood afar off. Then they said to Moses, "You speak with us, and we will hear; but let not God speak with us, lest we

die." And Moses said to the people, "Do not fear; for God has come to test you, and that His fear may be before you, so that you may not sin."

—EXODUS 20:18–20

Notice that the people trembled and drew back. They no longer wanted to hear God's audible voice. Neither did they want to look upon or be in the presence of His glory—they were unable to bear it.

Moses quickly warned them, "Do not fear . . . ," encouraging them back into God's presence as he explained that God had come to test them.

Why does God test us? To find out what is in our hearts? Absolutely not. He already knows what is hidden in our hearts. He tests us so that *we* might know what is in our hearts. What was the purpose of the test presented to the Israelites? For them to know whether or not they feared God. If they feared Him they would not sin. Sin results whenever we draw away from Him.

Moses said, "Do not fear." Then he said that God had come " . . . that His fear may be before you." This verse makes a distinction between *being afraid of God* and *fearing Him.* Moses feared God, but the people did not. It is an infallible truth that if we do not fear God, we will be afraid of Him at the revelation of His glory, for every knee shall bow to Him, if not out of godly fear then out of terror (2 Cor. 5:10–11).

> So the people stood afar off, but Moses drew near the thick darkness where God was.
>
> —EXODUS 20:21

Look at the difference in the responses to God's manifested glory: Israel drew back but Moses drew near. This illustrates the different responses of believers today.

SIMILAR IN MANY WAYS

IT IS IMPORTANT that we realize the Israelites were not so

very different from our modern church.

- *They all came out of Egypt,* which typifies salvation.
- *They all experienced and benefited from the miracles of God,* as have many in the church.
- *They all experienced deliverance from their oppressors,* which many have experienced today in the church.
- *They still desired their old lifestyle*—if they could have it without the bondage they experienced previously. How often we see this in the church today. People are saved and delivered, yet their hearts never leave the lifestyle of the world, although that lifestyle led them to bondage.
- *They experienced the wealth of the sinner that God had laid up for the just.* The Bible records: "He also brought them out with silver and gold . . . " (Ps. 105:37). Yet they used this blessing of God to build an idol! Have we done the same today? We hear of financial miracles, yet often those who are most blessed end up bestowing their affection and strength on material and financial blessings rather than upon the Lord who blessed them.
- *They experienced the healing power of God,* for when they left Egypt the Bible records: "There was none feeble among His tribes" (Ps. 105:37). That's even better than today's greatest miracle crusades. Moses left Egypt with three million strong, healthy people. Can you imagine a city of three million with no one sick or in the hospital? The Israelites had served under hardship for four hundred years. Imagine the healings and miracles which took place as they ate the Passover lamb!

The Israelites were no strangers to God's saving, healing, miracle-working, and delivering power. In fact, they celebrated passionately whenever God moved miraculously on their behalf. They danced and praised much like we do in our charismatic or Spirit-filled miracle services (Exod. 15:1, 20). It is interesting to note that the Israelites were drawn to His miraculous manifestations because they benefited from them, but were scared and drew back when His glory was revealed!

How different are we today? We are still drawn to miracles. People will travel miles and give big offerings, hoping to receive double portions from God in miracle services. But what will happen when God's glory is revealed? Then hearts will be exposed in His glorious presence. We can live with sin undetected around the miraculous, but sin cannot hide in the light of His revealed glory.

WHAT BLINDED THE PEOPLE

FORTY YEARS later, the older generation had died in the desert, and Moses reviewed for a new generation what had happened at the mountain where God revealed His glory.

> So it was, when you heard the voice from the midst of the darkness, while the mountain was burning with fire, that you came near to me, all the heads of your tribes and your elders. And you said: "Surely the Lord our God has shown us His glory and His greatness, and we have heard His voice from the midst of the fire. We have seen this day that God speaks with man; yet he still lives. Now therefore, why should we die? For this great fire will consume us; if we hear the voice of the Lord our God anymore, then we shall die. . . . You go near and hear all that the Lord our God may say, and tell us all that the Lord our God says to you, and we will hear and do it."
>
> —DEUTERONOMY 5:23–27

They cried out, "We cannot approach His glorious presence nor stand in the midst of Him and live." They wanted Moses to hear for them, and they promised to hear him and do whatever God said to do! They attempted to live by this pattern for thousands of years but could not obey His words. How different are we today? Do we get God's Word from our pastor and preachers but withdraw from the mountain of God? Are we afraid to hear His voice that lays bare the condition of our hearts? This heart condition is no different than that of the children of Israel.

Moses was very disappointed with Israel's response. He couldn't understand their lack of hunger for God's presence. How could they be so foolish? How could they be so blind? Moses brought his concerns before God in hope of a remedy to this condition. But see what happened:

> Then the Lord heard the voice of your words when you spoke to me, and the Lord said to me: "I have heard the voice of the words of this people which they have spoken to you. They are right in all that they have spoken."
> —DEUTERONOMY 5:28

I'm sure Moses was shocked at God's response. He must have thought, *What . . . the people are right? For once they are actually right! They really cannot come into the presence of God. Why?* God interrupted with the answer:

> Oh, that they had such a heart in them that they would fear Me and always keep all My commandments, that it might be well with them and with their children forever!
> —DEUTERONOMY 5:29

God lamented, "Oh, that they had such a heart in them that they would fear me . . . " They all could have been like Moses, reflecting God's glory and knowing His ways, if they had but possessed hearts that feared God as Moses did! But their hearts remained darkened and their minds blind to the very thing they so desperately needed.

What blinded them? The answer is clear: They did not have hearts that feared the Lord. This was evidenced by their disobedience to the commandments and Word of God. If we compare Moses with the children of Israel, we find the difference between the one who fears God and one who does not.

TREMBLING AT GOD'S WORD

A PERSON who fears God trembles at His Word and in His presence. (Isa. 66:2; Jer. 5:22). What does it mean to tremble at His Word? It can all be summed up in one statement:

> *To willingly obey God even when it appears more advantageous to compromise or not obey His Word.*

Our hearts must be firmly established in the fact that God is good. He is not a child-abuser. A person who fears God knows this, for he knows God's character. That is why he or she will draw near to God even when others would draw back in terror.

That person realizes that any immediate or impending difficulty encountered at God's hand will ultimately bring forth good in the end. Most would mentally agree with this, yet in times of hardship what we *truly believe* is clearly revealed. Only then will we see our faith for what it is by the light of the fire of trials.

The hardships that Israel faced exposed the contents of their hearts. Let's examine their different responses to God's Word. The children of Israel would obey God's Word as long as they saw the immediate benefit for them. But the moment they suffered or could no longer see the benefits, they lost sight of God and complained bitterly.

For centuries Israel had prayed and cried for deliverance from their Egyptian oppressors. They longed to return to the land of promise. God sent their deliverer, Moses. The Lord told Moses, "I have come down to deliver them out of the hand of the Egyptians, and to bring them up from that land to a good and large land, to a land flowing with milk and honey" (Exod. 3:8).

Moses went before Pharaoh and proclaimed God's words to "let His people go." But Pharaoh responded by increasing their hardship. No longer would straw be provided for the overwhelming tally of bricks the Israelite slaves were to produce. They would have to glean by night and labor by day. The total number of bricks could not diminish although their straw had been removed. God's word of freedom had increased their suffering. They complained under this oppression and told Moses to "leave us alone and quit preaching to Pharaoh; you are making life worse for us."

When God finally did deliver them from Egypt, Pharaoh's heart was hardened again, and He pursued the Israelites into the wilderness with his finest chariots and warriors. When the Hebrews saw that Egypt had rallied against them and they were backed up to the Red Sea, they again complained. "Is this not the word that we told you in Egypt, saying, 'Let us alone that we may serve the Egyptians?' For *it would have been better for us* to serve the Egyptians than that we should die in the wilderness" (Exod. 14:12, emphasis added).

Notice the words, "It would have been better for us." In essence, they were saying, "Why should we obey God when it is only making our lives miserable? We are worse off—not better." They were quick to compare their former lifestyle with their present condition. Whenever the two did not balance, the Israelites wanted to go back. They desired comfort over obedience to God's will. Oh, how they lacked the fear of God! They did not tremble at His Word.

God split the sea, and the children of Israel crossed on dry land and saw their oppressors buried. They celebrated God's goodness and danced and praised before Him. They were certain they would never again doubt His goodness! But they did not know their own hearts. Another test would arise and again expose their unfaithfulness. Just three days later they complained again that they did not want bitter water, but sweet. (See Exodus 15:22–25.)

How often do we do the same? We want soft and pleasant words when the bitter is what's necessary for cleansing us from impurities. That is why Solomon said, "But to a hungry soul every bitter thing is sweet" (Prov. 27:7).

A few days passed and the children of Israel again complained about the lack of food. They said, "Oh, that we had died by the hand of the Lord in the land of Egypt" (Exod. 16:1–4). Can you see how religiously they were behaving?

Again the Israelites complained of a lack of sweet water

(Exod. 17:1–4). Over and over, they complained whenever they encountered a new hardship. As long as it looked good for them, they kept God's Word. But if obedience meant hardship, the Israelites quickly complained.

A DIFFERENT HEART

MOSES WAS quite different. His heart had been tested long before. We are told:

> By faith Moses, when he became of age, refused to be called the son of Pharaoh's daughter, choosing rather to suffer affliction with the people of God than to enjoy the passing pleasures of sin, esteeming the reproach of Christ greater riches than the treasures in Egypt; for he looked to the reward.
>
> —HEBREWS 11:24–26

The children of Israel did not choose their bondage. Moses had been presented with the finest of everything the world could offer but refused it all to suffer affliction with God's people. His was quite a different attitude from that of the children of Israel. They wanted to return to Egypt (the world), having quickly forgotten its oppression. They only remembered that they had feasted on the things they now lacked in the wilderness of God's testing. Moses chose hardship, " . . . for he looked to the reward." What reward was he looking for? We find the answer in Exodus, chapter 33.

> Then the Lord said to Moses, "Depart and go up from here, you and the people whom you have brought out of the land of Egypt, to the land of which I swore to Abraham, Isaac, and Jacob, saying, 'To your descendants I will give it.' And I will send My Angel before you, and I will drive out the Canaanite and the Amorite and the Hittite and the Perizzite and the Hivite and the Jebusite. Go up to a land flowing with milk and honey; for I will not

go up in your midst, lest I consume you on the way, for you are a stiff-necked people."

—EXODUS 33:1–3

God told Moses to go down and take the people to the land He had promised them, the very land they had waited hundreds of years to inherit. God even promised Moses the escort of a choice angel, although He would not accompany them.

But Moses quickly responded: "If Your Presence does not go with us, do not bring us up from here" (Exod. 33:15).

I am glad that the option of entering the Promised Land without God was not placed before the children of Israel. If they would have chosen a comfortable life in Egypt over God, they surely would have chosen the Promised Land without Him. They probably would have had a party and left without a second thought! But Moses had not set his sights on the Promised Land, so his response was different.

Moses said, "The promise is nothing without Your presence!" He refused God's offer because his reward was the presence of the Lord. Think of the position Moses was in when he responded, "Do not bring us up from here." Where was "here"? The desert!

Moses lived under the same conditions as the rest of Israel. He wasn't endowed with super-human ability that exempted him from the hardships the rest of Israel experienced. He thirsted and hungered the same as they, yet we never see him complaining with the others. He was offered an "out" from this suffering and the opportunity to go to the land of his dreams, but he refused.

One method God will use to test us is making us an offer He expects us to refuse. The offer may initially promise greater success, but at what price? It may even look as though our ministry will expand and go further. But in the depths of our hearts we know that to choose it would be against God's ultimate desire. Only those who tremble at His Word would choose that which appears less beneficial.

In 2 Kings, chapter 2, Elijah told Elisha three times to stay put. Each order was yet another test. It would have been easier for Elisha to stay, but Elisha insisted, "As the Lord lives, and as your soul lives, I will not leave you!" (2 Kings 2:2). He knew the heavenly reward was far more important than his temporary comfort!

ALIKE OUTWARDLY, DIFFERENT INWARDLY

OUTWARDLY, or physically, you could not tell the difference between Moses and the children of Israel. They were all descendants of Abraham. They had all left Egypt under intervention of God's miraculous power. They were all positioned to inherit God's promises. All professed to know and serve Jehovah. The difference was hidden in the inner recesses of their hearts. Moses feared God; therefore, he perceived God's heart and ways. But because the children of Israel did not fear God, they were blinded, and their understanding was darkened.

It is no different today. Christianity has become almost a club. You remember what a club is all about from when you were a child. You'd join clubs because you wanted to belong. In the safety of a club, you were unified with the other members because of a common interest or cause. It felt good to be a part of something bigger than yourself. The club was behind you and gave you a sense of security.

There are many professing Christians who no more fear God than those who have never set foot in the church. As secure members of the Christianity club, why should they be afraid? As a matter of fact, demons tremble more than some in the church. James warned those who professed salvation but who lacked the fear of God, "You believe that there is one God. You do well. Even the demons believe—and tremble!" (James 2:19).

These people sit in our churches, work on ministry staffs, and preach from the pulpits. They come from all walks of life, ranging from ghettos to the Hollywood fast lane. They confess salvation and love God's promises, but they are shortsighted— and like the children of Israel, they do not fear God.

Jude foresaw this day and warned that people would attend our churches and profess salvation by God's grace, due to membership in the Christianity club. They would attend believers' gatherings and participate without fear, all the while serving only themselves (Jude 1:12).

In Matthew 7:21–23, Jesus said there would be those who would cast out devils, and do other wonders in His name, calling Him Lord and Savior, yet neglecting to live in obedience to the will of God. Jesus described this condition as "tares growing among wheat." You would not easily be able to tell the difference between the wheat and the tares. Just as with Israel, the fire of God's glorious presence will ultimately expose the contents of every heart. This will be the church's condition upon entering the season of harvest (Matt. 13:26).

Malachi prophesied that in these last days God would send a prophetic voice—as He did with Samuel, Moses, and John the Baptist—to prepare His people for His glory. It would not be one, however, but many prophetic messengers. These messengers would arise with such a unity of purpose that they would speak as one man, calling for those who are deceived to return with all their hearts to the Lord.

Thus, divine order will be restored in the hearts of God's people. These prophets are not messengers of judgment, but of mercy. Through them, the Lord calls to His own to escape judgment. Malachi records:

> Behold, I send My messenger, and he will prepare the way before Me. And the Lord, whom you seek, will suddenly come to His temple . . . But who can endure the day of His coming? And who can stand when He appears? For He is like a refiner's fire and like launderers' soap.
>
> —MALACHI 3:1–2

Malachi is not describing the catching away of the church. He says that the Lord will come to—not for His temple. Hosea said that after two thousand years the Lord would come to us, His temple, as the latter rain. That speaks of His manifested glory. Malachi then asks, "But who can endure His glorious coming to His temple?" Both prophets confirm that this event is not the same as the catching away of the church.

Malachi answers his own question, presenting two outcomes of God's glorious presence. First it is to refine and purify those who fear Him (vv. 3, 16–17). Second, it will judge the hearts of those who *say* they serve Him but in reality *do not fear Him* (vv. 3:5; 4:1). Once this purification occurs, he tells us:

> Then you shall again discern between the righteous and the wicked, between one who serves God and one who does not serve Him.
>
> —MALACHI 3:18

Before the glory was manifested, you could not tell the one who serves God from the one who merely provides lip service to the Lord. Hypocrisy cannot hide from the light of God's glory. The club mentality will finally be gone. This lends a better understanding of Jesus' stern warning for the New Testament believer:

> And I say to you, My friends, do not be afraid of those who kill the body, and after that have no more that they can do. But I will show you whom you should fear: Fear Him who, after He has killed, has power to cast into hell; yes, I say to you, fear Him!
>
> —LUKE 12:4–5

The fear of God keeps us from the destructive path of the deceived. Moses said that the fear of God in the hearts of His people is the strength to walk free from sin (Exod. 20:20). Solomon wrote, "By the fear of the Lord one departs from evil" (Prov. 16:6). Jesus warned the believers for a specific purpose, and preceded His exhortation to fear God with a warning about the deceptive trap of hypocrisy:

> For there is nothing covered that will not be revealed, nor hidden that will not be known.
>
> —LUKE 12:2

When we cover or hide sin to protect our reputations, we place a veil over our hearts. We mistakenly think this veil causes us to appear pure, when actually we are not. This ultimately leads to hypocrisy. So now we not only deceive others but ourselves. (See 2 Timothy 3:13.) As with the children of Israel, we are blinded and cannot see.

The fear of God is our only protection from hypocrisy. Then we will not hide sin in our hearts, because we will fear God more than the opinions of mortal men. We will become more concerned with what God thinks of us than what man thinks. We will be more concerned with God's desires than with our temporary comfort. We will esteem His Word more valuable than man's. We will turn our hearts to the Lord! And Paul says:

> Nevertheless when one turns to the Lord, the veil is taken away.
>
> —2 CORINTHIANS 3:16

THE FEAR OF THE LORD
WILL KEEP US FROM
COMPROMISING GOD'S
TRUTH FOR THE PURSUIT OF
PERSONAL GAIN.

Twelve

FROM GLORY TO GLORY

Nevertheless when one turns to the Lord, the veil is taken away.
—2 CORINTHIANS 3:16

WHAT A powerful promise! When we turn to the Lord, any veil screening us from beholding His glory is removed!

Before I go any further, I want to emphasize the full implication and meaning of this scripture. We need to qualify this statement, because often the full impact of what Paul is saying can be lost through the cloud of our present "Christianity club" mentality.

Jesus proposed a startling question, one we often skip and bypass today. He asked, "Why do you call Me 'Lord, Lord,' and not do the things which I say?" (Luke 6:46). The Greek word for "Lord" is *kurios*. It means "supreme in authority." It also carries the connotation of ownership.

The Lord is the creator, ruler, and owner of the universe. As Supreme Authority, He placed man, with delegated authority, in the garden. Man turned over his delegated dominion of the earth to Satan (Luke 4:6). At the cross, Jesus redeemed back what was lost. Now we have a choice. We can relinquish complete ownership of our lives to Jesus, or retain it and remain trapped under the dominion of a lost and dying world. There is no third option, no middle ground, no in between.

When we do not fear God and honor Him as Lord, we withhold a portion of the control of our lives. We may confess Jesus as Lord, but our irreverence is made clear by the fruit of our lives. If we fear God we will yield completely to His authority as King and Lord. This allows Him full and unrestricted possession of us. We become His bondservants.

Paul, Timothy, James, Peter, and Jude were all referred to in the epistles as bondservants. (See Romans 1:1; Colossians 4:12; James 1:1; 2 Peter 1:1; Jude 1.) A bondservant freely gives himself in service in repayment of a debt. It is not slavery, for a slave has no choice in the matter. Bond-servitude is voluntary. We serve out of love, trust, and reverential fear of God. We willingly give Him complete, unconditional ownership of our lives.

This is why Paul could bravely face the chains, tribulations, and hardships that awaited him in every city. He could say with determination, "And see, now I go bound in the spirit to Jerusalem" (Acts 20:22). Did the Lord bind Paul? Absolutely not! Paul understood that in fulfilling the will of God, he would suffer. But Paul had chosen God's desire over his own comfort. He had freely given total and unconditional ownership of his life to Jesus.

Paul referred to the extreme hardships he would encounter with these words: "But none of these things move me; nor do I count my life dear to myself, so that I may finish my race with joy" (Acts 20:24). He was committed no matter the cost. Only our combined love for God and holy fear of Him fulfill our response to His lordship. This is the commitment required of all those who follow Him (Luke 14:25–33).

When Jesus questioned, "Why do you call Me 'Lord, Lord,' and not do the things which I say?" He was actually saying, "Do not deceive yourself by calling Me 'Lord' while you continue to live your life as if you owned it."

THE VEIL OF DECEPTION

KING SAUL'S life exemplifies this concept. God sent Saul a command through the prophet Samuel. Saul was instructed to gather his army and attack Amalek, utterly destroying everything that breathed—every man, woman, child, and animal.

Saul didn't refuse Samuel's instructions with, "Absolutely not!" and stomp off in the opposite direction. That would be obvious disobedience. Rather, Saul listened, gathered his army, and attacked Amalek. In this attack, tens of thousands of men, women, and children were killed. Saul spared only the Amalekite king. Perhaps he wanted another king as a trophy to serve in his palace.

Most likely thousands of animals were killed as well. Saul saved only a few of the best sheep, lambs, and oxen. He reasoned that the people could sacrifice these to the Lord, and even that it was "scriptural." To an observer who had not heard the prophet's word, Saul might have appeared to be a godly king. "Look, he sacrifices only the very best to the Lord!"

After this campaign God spoke to Samuel: "I greatly regret that I have set up Saul as king, for he has turned back from following Me, and has not performed My commandments" (1 Sam. 15:11).

The next day Samuel went to confront Saul. When Saul saw Samuel coming, he greeted him excitedly with the salutation, "Blessed are you of the Lord! I have performed the commandment of the Lord" (1 Sam. 15:13).

Wait a minute! That was definitely not God's impression! We just read His opinion. What's happened here? How could there be such differing views of the same incident? Saul really believed he obeyed God. How could there be such a variance? James explains it:

> But be doers of the word, and not hearers only, deceiving yourselves.
>
> —JAMES 1:22

When we hear God's word and do not do it, we deceive our

own hearts! This is how someone can really believe they're obedient to God when in reality they're acting in disobedience. This is both a fearful and sobering revelation! Deception veils the heart and obstructs the truth. The more a person disobeys, the thicker and more obstructive the veil becomes, making it harder to remove.

Allow me to reiterate some important points. First, Saul did not stomp off and refuse to do as he was told. He went. Second, he killed tens of thousands of people, sparing only one. He killed all but a few of the thousands of animals. He probably did 99 percent of what he was told to do. Yet God called his nearly complete obedience—*rebellion* (v. 23)!

Today we would say, "That's all right; it was a good effort." We may even defend Saul, pointing out, "After all, he did do *almost* everything. Give him credit for what he *did* do right! Why point out the one thing he didn't do? Look at all he did! Don't be so hard on poor Saul!"

In God's eyes, partial or selective obedience is the same as rebellion to His authority. It is the evidence of a lack of the fear of God!

Once I was in Canada preparing to minister. We were in the middle of praise and worship when the Spirit of the Lord posed this question: "Do you know what a religious spirit is?"

Although I have written and preached on religious spirits and how they operate, I knew right away that my information must have been limited at best. I have learned that anytime God asks a question, He is not looking for information. I answered, "No, Lord—please tell me."

He quickly responded, "A person with a religious spirit is one who uses My Word to execute his own will!" In other words, it is when we take what the Lord has said and work our own desires into it.

I stood in awe of the wisdom imparted by the Spirit of God. I applied this to the situation with Saul. I could see how Saul had done what He was told, yet worked his own desires into it. God's heart was not his focus. Saul had seen an opportunity to benefit himself and strengthen his position with the people, and he seized it. Is that lordship? Is that trembling at God's Word? The fear of the Lord will keep us from compromising God's truth for the pursuit of personal gain. Then we will obey God's Word, no matter the cost.

WHAT MIRROR ARE YOU BEHOLDING?

HEAR AGAIN the words of James:

> But be doers of the word, and not hearers only, deceiving yourselves. For if anyone is a hearer of the word and not a doer, he is like a man observing his natural face in a mirror; for he observes himself, goes away, and immediately forgets what kind of man he was.
>
> —JAMES 1:22–24

James uses this natural example to illustrate what actually happens in the spirit when we are not submitted to the lordship of Jesus. When we do not tremble at His Word with unconditional obedience, it is like looking at ourselves in the mirror then walking away as if we hadn't looked and going back because we have forgotten what we look like. We can see as long as we are looking in the mirror, but as soon as we walk away, we forget, as though we were blind.

This explains why people can read, listen, and even preach the Word of God, yet live like those who do not know God's Word. There is very little change in their lives. Virtually no transformation has taken place. The psalmist describes the condition of those who attend the house of God, hear His Word, and yet remain unchanged. He says, "Because they do not change, therefore they do not fear God" (Ps. 55:19).

These people confess to be saved, yet remain unchanged by God's power. They are unholy, unthankful, unloving, disobedient, and unforgiving, and exhibit other traits as well that make them no different from one who has never heard God's Word. They probably do not smoke, drink, or swear like the heathen on the streets, but inside their motives are the same—

self-seeking. Paul described their condition as continuously learning but never able to apply the knowledge of the truth. They would be deceived (2 Tim. 3:1–7, 13).

In the desert, the children of Israel suffered this shortsightedness of a veiled heart. The veil was called *deception*. They heard God's Word and saw His mighty power, yet remained very much the same. Their lack of holy fear caused their spiritual eyes to be darkened.

Without true repentance, this veil thickened to the point of blindness. Their hearts were blinded to the manner of persons they had become. While they celebrated deliverance from Egypt (the world), they lost touch with the purposes of God and drew back—even cowered—when His glorious presence was revealed. The same could happen to us if we do not heed God's warnings.

Paul tells us what will happen when we are submitted to the lordship of Jesus, fearing His presence, and trembling at His Word.

> Nevertheless when one turns to the Lord, the veil is taken away. But we all, with unveiled face, beholding as in a mirror the glory of the Lord, are being transformed into the same image from glory to glory, just as by the Spirit of the Lord.
>
> —2 CORINTHIANS 3:16–18

As with James, Paul used the analogy of looking into a mirror. Yet it is not a natural image we behold, but the very glory of God which is seen in the face of Jesus Christ (2 Cor. 4:6). This image is revealed in our hearts when we not only *hear* His Word but are obedient to *do* it. James confirms this:

> But he who looks carefully into the faultless law, the [law] of liberty, and is faithful to it and perseveres in looking into it, being not a heedless listener who forgets but an active doer [who obeys], he shall be blessed in his doing (in his life of obedience).
>
> —JAMES 1:25, AMP

The perfect law of liberty is Jesus. He is the living, revealed Word of God. John tells us, "For there are three that bear witness in heaven: the Father, the Word, and the Holy Spirit; and these three are one" (1 John 5:7).

When we diligently seek Jesus, remain attentive to His Word under the leadership of the Holy Spirit, and obey what is revealed, our eyes remain clear and unveiled. Then we can perceive His glory!

Remember, His desire is for us to behold His glory! He lamented when Israel could not stand in His glorious presence due to their lack of godly fear. Only those with unveiled hearts can behold Him!

As we behold His glory in the mirror of His revealed Word, we are changed into His image by the Spirit of God! Glory to God! Now you can understand the urgency felt by the writer of Hebrews:

> Therefore we must give the more earnest heed to the things we have heard, lest we drift away.
> —HEBREWS 2:1

There is a high calling for every believer—to be conformed to the glorious image of Jesus Christ (Phil. 3:14; Rom. 8:29). But if we are not diligent to obey God's Word, we will unwittingly drift from His course set before us. Can you imagine attempting to drive while blindfolded? You could turn on the ignition but in no time your car would veer from its destination! You can't see where you are going if you are blindfolded. Obedience to God keeps your eyes uncovered!

THE GUIDING LIGHT OF OUR ENTIRE BEING

WE ARE changed into what we behold. If there is a veil over our spiritual eyes, then our image of the Lord is distorted. In our minds, His image takes on the form of corruptible man rather than the incorruptible God He really is. We then view His ways by the dim light of the culture in which we live. This is why

Israel could experience mighty miracles and manifestations, yet quickly find themselves behaving like the nations who knew not the Lord. Jesus said:

> The lamp of the body is the eye. If therefore your eye is good, your whole body will be full of light. But if your eye is bad, your whole body will be full of darkness. If therefore the light that is in you is darkness, how great is that darkness!
> —MATTHEW 6:22–23

The lamp that gives direction to our body (our being) is the eye. This image of the lamp speaks not just of physical sight, but also of the eyes of the heart (Eph. 1:18). Our entire being follows its perception and directions. If our eyes behold the living Word of God (Heb. 6:5), our entire being is filled with the light of God's nature (1 John 1:5). We are continually transformed in this light of truth; we are safe and will not drift off course.

Jesus went on to say that eyes focused on evil would have their entire being flooded with the nature of darkness. This describes the darkened heart of an unbeliever.

But look closely at His last statement: "If therefore the light [which is your perception of Jesus] that is in you is darkness, how great is that darkness" (Matt. 6:33)! This statement is not made to an unbeliever, but to the person who knows God's Word. The light is in him. Jesus is saying that if our perception is darkened or veiled due to a lack of holy fear, this darkness will actually be greater than the darkness that shrouds those who have never seen or heard the truth. (See Jude 1:12–13 and Luke 12:47–48.)

Recall God's words to those who claimed to know Him, yet lacked the fear of Him: "What right have you to declare My statutes, or take My covenant in your mouth, seeing you hate instruction and cast My words behind you?" (Ps. 50:16–17). They are those who confess their belief in His Word and even preach it, but the light that is in them is great darkness. With veiled eyes they see God as they see themselves, instead of seeing Him as who He really is. God says, "These things you have done, and I kept silent; you thought that I was altogether like you" (v. 21).

WORK OUT YOUR SALVATION

PETER ENCOURAGES us that God has "given to us exceedingly great and precious promises, that through these you may be partakers of the divine nature, having escaped the corruption that is in the world through lust" (2 Pet. 1:2–4). "Partakers of the divine nature!" What a promise!

He explains that the fulfillment of this promise would be both conditional and progressive. For he says, "You do well to heed as a light that shines in a dark place, until the day dawns and the morning star rises in your hearts" (2 Pet. 1:19). The condition: Heed the exceeding great and precious promises. The progression: As we tremble and obey, then the light of His glory will grow. It begins as the strength of dawn and continues from glory to glory until it shines as the sun in full strength. Proverbs 4:18 tells us, "The path of the just is like the shining sun, that shines ever brighter unto the perfect day." In the perfect day we shall shine as the sun forever (Matt. 13:43). We will not *reflect* His glory—but *emit* it! Hallelujah!

As we behold the glory of the Lord in the mirror of His revealed Word, we are "being transformed [changed] into the same image of the Lord from glory to glory." This describes the process the Bible calls "working out" our salvation. Paul gives specific instructions on this to the Philippians. As you read his instructions, ponder the fact that if these same instructions had been heeded by Israel, they would have been spared the undesirable fate of perishing in the wilderness.

> Therefore, my beloved, as you have always obeyed, not as in my presence only, but now much more in my absence, work out your own salvation with fear and trembling; for it is God who works in you both to will and to do for His good pleasure.
>
> —PHILIPPIANS 2:12–13

I know this letter is from Paul to the Philippians, but it represents a letter to us from the Lord. All Scripture is given by the inspiration of the Holy Spirit, and there is no private interpretation. We should read this verse as though God spoke it to us personally. Before proceeding, read Philippians 2:12–13 again in this light.

These verses illustrate how the fear of God strengthens us to obey Him, not only in His presence but also in the absence of His presence. The Scriptures describe two different aspects of the presence of God. First, there is His omnipresence. Simply put, *God is everywhere.* David described it thus: "Where can I flee from your presence? If I go yo to the heavens, you are there; if I make my bed in the depths [hell] you are there" (Ps. 139:7–8, NIV). This is the presence He promises will never leave us or forsake us (Heb. 13:5).

Second, there is God's tangible—or manifest—presence. This is when His presence becomes real to us in this natural world. We sense His love often during services; we sense His warmth as we worship; we sense His power as we pray. It is easy to obey God during these times when our prayers have just been answered, His promises fulfilled, and joy abounds. But a person who fears God is one who will obey even in rough times when there is no tangible presence of God to encourage.

UNWAVERING FEAR OF GOD

CONSIDER JOSEPH, Abraham's great-grandson. In a dream God showed Joseph that he would be a great leader, ruling even over his brothers! But what happened immediately after receiving this promise? The brothers Joseph was destined to rule one day became jealous and threw him into a pit. Many today would wonder in shock, "How could God allow this? Was this dream just a big tease?" After the initial shock, they would become offended with God. Their offense is another manifestation of a lack of holy fear! Yet, we find no record of Joseph's complaining.

These same brothers sold Joseph as a slave to a foreign nation.

He served in the house of Potiphar, an idol worshiper, for more than ten years. Ten years—think of it! Each day his dream from God must have appeared more distant and futile. Today, most of us would be beyond questioning God after ten years; we would have already given up! Yet still we find no evidence of Joseph's complaining. He did not abandon his hope, forget his dream, or yield to discouragement. He feared God.

In contrast, the children of Israel indulged themselves with complaining and grumbling. Joseph's patience endured for ten years of slavery while the patience of the Israelites waned after a few months. Today many of us complain when our prayers aren't answered within a few weeks. How different we are from Joseph, don't you agree?

Joseph was isolated and alone in a pagan land far from all he'd known and loved. He had no fellowship with believers. There was no brother to confide in. In this state of loneliness, his master's wife attempted to seduce Joseph. Draped in silks and scented with the finest oils of Egypt, Potiphar's wife daily pleaded with Joseph to lie with her.

I love the way Joseph demonstrated his fear of God. Although he had experienced hardship and disappointment, he did not yield to Potiphar's wife. If he had lost his godly fear and become offended with God, he would have lacked the strength to withstand temptation. He rebuffed Potiphar's wife: "How then can I do this great wickedness, and sin against God?" (Gen. 39:9).

Joseph's obedience to God landed him in Pharaoh's dungeon. At this point, how many would still choose to trust and obey God? Many would fall prey to the death grip of bitterness. (See Hebrews 12:15.) Joseph remained in prison for more than two years. Yet, we still find no evidence of his complaining or becoming embittered. Even in the darkness of prison and the confines of chains, Joseph continued to fear God! No disappointment could turn his heart from God.

What is most powerful is that in all his sorrow Joseph still ministered to his fellow prisoners. During hardship he comforted them, interpreting their dreams and telling them about Jehovah.

COMPLAINING: THE TRANSFORMATION-STOPPER

JOSEPH'S descendants were very different. They obeyed when their desires were met and when God manifested His mighty power on their behalf. Whenever they were discouraged or felt abandoned, they quickly drifted into disobedience. The first symptom of such drifting always came in the form of complaining.

Those offended with God usually are not so foolish as to directly oppose Him. Instead, they resist His Word or leadership. The children of Israel complained about their leaders, but Moses answered with, "Your complaints are not against us but against the Lord" (Exod. 16:8).

Complaining is a killer. It will short-circuit the life of God in you faster than almost any other thing! Complaining indirectly communicates to the Lord, "I don't like what You are doing in my life—and if I were You, I would do it differently." Complaining is nothing more than a manifestation of insubordination to God's authority. It is extremely irreverent! God hates it! Joseph feared God, and he never complained. That is why the Lord admonishes us:

> Work out your own salvation with fear and trembling; for it is God who works in you both to will and to do for His good pleasure. Do all things without complaining and disputing.
> —PHILIPPIANS 2:12–14

God sternly warns us not to allow complaining to take root in our hearts. We are not left helpless by its intense attack. The fear of the Lord is a force within us that will keep that killer out. Proverbs confirms this:

> The fear of the Lord is a fountain of life, to turn one away from the snares of death.
> —PROVERBS 14:27

Joseph lived in a spiritual desert for more than twelve years. It appeared that nothing was going his way. There was nothing to strengthen and encourage him. But there was a fountain from which Joseph drew—one deep within. This fountain provided the strength he needed to obey God in tough, dry times. It was the fear of God!

He was able to avoid the pitfalls of hatred, offense, jealousy, resentment, anger, and adultery through the life-giving waters of that fountain. When others would have fallen into the traps of death, Joseph was able to turn away and minister to others—even in his darkest hours.

Joseph was wise in his behavior because he feared God. "The fear of the Lord is the instruction of wisdom" (Prov. 15:33). Those who fear God are wise. Daniel points out:

> Those who are wise shall shine like the brightness of the firmament, and those who turn many to righteousness like the stars forever and ever.
>
> —DANIEL 12:3

Joseph passed the ultimate heart test by giving of himself and declaring God's faithfulness in his darkest hour. It wasn't long before Joseph's wisdom caused him to shine brightly in Egypt. His virtue could not be hidden but was revealed to an entire pagan nation.

Interestingly, it was Joseph's behavior while in prison, and his response to his fellow prisoners, that eventually led to his promotion. In Genesis 40, we read that the Pharaoh's chief butler and chief baker were among the prisoners. Both had dreams, which were interpreted by Joseph. To the butler, Joseph proclaimed the meaning of the dream:

> "This is the interpretation of it: The three branches are three days. Now within three days Pharaoh will lift up your head and restore you to your place, and you will put Pharaoh's cup in his hand according to the former manner, when you were his butler."
>
> —GENESIS 40:12–13

But to the baker, the interpretation was not so good.

> So Joseph answered and said, "This is the interpretation of it:
> The three baskets are three days. Within three days Pharaoh
> will lift off your head from you and hang you on a tree; and
> the birds will eat your flesh from you."
> —GENESIS 40:18–19

If there had been a morsel of complaint in Joseph's heart, he would not have ministered to either the butler or the baker. If he hadn't ministered to them, he would have remained in prison until his death.

In his final moments, Joseph would have still been murmuring about what appeared to be God's unfaithfulness, when in reality God's promise would have been aborted because of Joseph's lack of godly fear. But God was faithful to release Joseph from his prison chains. At the appointed time, Joseph was summoned by the Pharaoh himself to interpret a dream, at the recommendation of none other than the chief butler. And an entire nation was delivered from famine because one man—Joseph—feared the Lord.

In the latter half of the twentieth century, the church has displayed a lack of the fear of God. Therefore, we are viewed as a reproach rather than as shining stars before our nation in need. Our sins are frequently broadcast by the media, and we have lost the respect that believers should have. We have not demonstrated the faithful, God-fearing qualities found in Joseph. May God help us with His grace!

SHINING FORTH HIS GLORY

JOB WAS another man who suffered greatly. He too was sorely tested. He tried to make sense of all that he suffered but fell into despair. His friends came to counsel him but their words did not help matters and only added to Job's confusion. He searched for wisdom but it eluded him. God was silent while Job and his friends shared their futile attempts to understand His ways. God waited until all their opinions were exhausted. He sent a preacher with wisdom named Elihu. But after this:

> Then the Lord answered Job out of the whirlwind, and said: "Who is this who darkens counsel by words without knowledge? Now prepare yourself like a man; I will question you, and you shall answer Me. Where were you when I laid the foundations of the earth? Tell Me, if you have understanding.
> —JOB 38:1–4

God expounds on and on, until Job is overwhelmed by God's awesome wisdom, understanding, and strength. Job is overcome with holy fear, and he cries out:

> I know that You can do everything, and that no purpose of Yours can be withheld from You. You asked, "Who is this who hides counsel without knowledge?" Therefore I have uttered what I did not understand, things too wonderful for me, which I did not know . . . I have heard of You by the hearing of the ear, but now my eye sees You. Therefore I abhor myself, and repent in dust and ashes.
> —JOB 42:2–6

Job feared God. He saw God. He was transformed. His physical pain and loss had not decreased but a greater sense of holy fear had been imparted. That fear contained the wisdom Job needed. Just as Joseph had ministered in his pain and hurt, Job turned and ministered to others.

> And the Lord restored Job's losses when he prayed for his friends. Indeed the Lord gave Job twice as much as he had before. . . . So Job died, old and full of days.
> —JOB 42:10, 17

Job shone forth with greater wisdom and strength than ever before. Many people today continue to glean from his pain and wisdom. We can see why God strongly warns us:

> Do all things without grumbling and faultfinding and com-
> plaining [against God] and questioning and doubting
> [among yourselves].
> —PHILIPPIANS 2:14, AMP

What gives us the ability to walk free of these killers? The fear
of God. When we fear God, our hearts are unveiled. As we
behold His glory, we are transformed into the image we behold.

> That you may become blameless and harmless, children of
> God without fault in the midst of a crooked and perverse
> generation, among whom you shine as lights in the world,
> holding fast the word of life . . .
> —PHILIPPIANS 2:15–16

The Amplified Bible says it like this:

> Among whom you are seen as bright lights (stars or beacons
> shining out clearly) in the [dark] world.
> —PHILIPPIANS 2:15, AMP

Glory to God forever! We who fear God are continually conformed to His image until we shine as brilliant lights in a dark
world. This describes the awesome glory His faithful church
shall emit in these last days.

In the previous chapter we discussed how this transformation
would escalate until God's glory in us will manifest so strongly
that sinners will be drawn to Christ by our light. Reviewing what
Isaiah said, we find:

> Arise, shine; for your light has come! And the glory of the
> Lord is risen upon you. For behold, the darkness shall cover
> the earth, and deep darkness the people; but the Lord will
> arise over you, and His glory will be seen upon you. The
> Gentiles shall come to your light, and kings to the bright-
> ness of your rising.
> —ISAIAH 60:1–3

God will manifest His glory in this earth. He has already said how He will do it. "I will glorify the house of My glory" (Isa. 60:7). The house of His glory is His people, His temple, those of us who fear and love Him. Zechariah foresaw the glory of the Lord arising on His people and said:

> Thus says the Lord of hosts: "In those days ten men from every language of the nations shall grasp the sleeve of a Jewish man [a believer], saying, 'Let us go with you, for we have heard that God is with you.'"
> —ZECHARIAH 8:23

Zechariah did not use the terminology we use today. So he could not say that men would grasp the sleeve of every Christian. He saw our day and described it in his own terms. What is most exciting is that we are rapidly approaching these days! Hallelujah!

TO FEAR GOD IS TO BELIEVE GOD.
TO BELIEVE GOD IS TO OBEY HIM.

Thirteen

FRIENDSHIP WITH GOD

The secret of the Lord is with those who fear Him, and He will show them His covenant.

—PSALM 25:14

NOW WE will discuss what I believe is the most exciting facet of walking in the fear of God. It is the heart's desire of every true believer. It is the only thing that will ever bring lasting fulfillment. It is God's motive for creation and purpose in redemption, the very focus of His heart, and a treasure reserved for those who fear Him. By way of introduction, let's turn to Solomon's wisdom:

Fear of the Lord is the beginning of knowledge.

—PROVERBS 1:7

The knowledge of what? Is Solomon referring to scientific knowledge? No, many scientists exalt man and have no fear of God. Does this verse refer to social or political accomplishment? No, for the world's ways are foolishness to God. Is it knowledge of the Scriptures? No, for although the Pharisees were experts in the law, they were displeasing to God. Our answer is found in Proverbs 2:5: "Fear the Lord, and you will gain knowledge of God." Let me put it to you in simpler terms: You will come to know God intimately. The psalmist confirms this by saying:

> The secret of the Lord is with those who fear Him.
> —Psalm 25:14

The fear of the Lord is the beginning, or starting place, of an intimate relationship with God. Intimacy is a two-way relationship. For example, I know *about* the president of the United States. I can list information about his accomplishments and his political stance, but I do not actually *know* Him. I lack a personal relationship with him. Those in the president's immediate family and his close associates *know* him. If we were in the same room, I would quickly recognize the president, but he would not know me. Although I'm a citizen of the United States and know *about* him, I could not speak to him as though he were my friend. That would be inappropriate and even disrespectful. I would still be under his jurisdiction and authority as president and under his protection as commander in chief, but his authority over me would not automatically grant me intimacy with him.

Another example would be those of us who are so taken with the athletic and Hollywood celebrities of our day. Their names are common in the households of America. The media has laid bare their personal lives through numerous television interviews and newspaper and magazine articles. I hear fans talk as though these celebrities were close friends. I have even seen people caught up emotionally in the marriage problems of their favorite celebrities and have watched them grieve as if they were a part of the family when their sports or screen heroes died.

If these fans ever met their celebrity hero on the street, they would not even receive a nod of acknowledgment. If they were bold enough to stop this celebrity, they may find the real person to be quite different from the image he or she portrays. The relationship between celebrities and their fans is a one-way relationship.

I have grieved over this same behavior in the church. I listen to believers talk about God as though He were just a buddy, someone they hang out with. They casually tell how God has shown them this or that. They say how much they desire His presence and hunger for His anointing. Often those young or not yet stable in their relationship with the Lord will feel uncomfortable and spiritually deficient around these "close friends" of God.

Within minutes you will usually hear these individuals contradict themselves. They will say something that clearly reveals that their relationship with God is not unlike that between a fan and his favorite celebrity. They prove to be expounding about a relationship that is just not there.

The Lord said we cannot even begin to know Him on intimate terms until we fear Him. In other words, an intimate relationship and friendship with God will not even begin until the fear of God is firmly planted in our hearts.

We can attend services, come forward in answer to every altar call, read our Bibles daily, and attend every prayer meeting. We can preach great and motivating sermons, work hard in the ministry for years, and even receive the respect and admiration of our peers. But if we do not fear God, we are only climbing the rungs of the religious ladder. What's the difference between these religious rituals and suffering from the celebrity syndrome?

I know people who can tell me more about a celebrity's personal life than they can tell me about their own. They are full of insight, scoop, facts, and details. Such knowledge of someone does not guarantee intimacy with them. These celebrity followers are like people who watch the lives of others through glass windows. They see the *what, where,* and *when,* but they do not know the *why.*

GOD'S FRIEND

GOD CALLED two men His friends in Scripture. This is not to say there were not others—only that God specifically acknowledged these two, intentionally recording their friendships. I believe He did this so we could benefit and receive insight into what God looks for in a friend.

The first is Abraham. Abraham was called the "friend of God" (2 Chron. 20:7). When Abraham was seventy-five years old, God came to Abraham and cut a covenant with him. Within the parameters of this covenant, God promised Abraham his heart's desire, a son. Before the birth of this son, Abraham made several mistakes—some that were quite serious.

Yet through it all, Abraham believed and obeyed God and was fully persuaded that God would perform all that was promised.

When Abraham was ninety-nine years of age, his wife became pregnant, and their promised son, Isaac, was born! Can you imagine the joy Abraham and Sarah experienced after waiting so many years? Can you imagine the love they had for this promised child?

THE TEST

TIME PASSED and this relationship grew as father and son became very close. The life of this boy meant more to Abraham than his own. His great wealth was nothing in comparison to the joy of this son. Nothing meant more to Abraham than this precious son given to him by God.

> Now it came to pass after these things that God tested Abraham, and said to him, "Abraham!" And he said, "Here I am." And He said, "Take now your son, your only son Isaac, whom you love, and go to the land of Moriah, and offer him there as a burnt offering on one of the mountains of which I shall tell you."
>
> —GENESIS 22:1–2

Can you imagine Abraham's shock at hearing these words? Never had he dreamed that God would ask such a hard thing of him. He was stunned. Father and son were so close. After all the years of waiting for this priceless young man, God had asked for more than even Abraham's own life—He had asked for his heart. It made no sense.

But Abraham knew that God did not make mistakes. There was no denying what God had already made clear. There were only two options for a covenant man—obey, or break covenant. To break covenant was not even a consideration for this man of faith, he was so immersed in godly fear.

We know it was a test, but Abraham did not. We never know God is testing us until we are on the other side of it. It may be possible to cheat on a university test, but no one can cheat on the exams God gives. If we have not studied and done our homework by purifying our hearts and cleansing our hands, we will not be able to pass God's tests, no matter how clever we are!

If Abraham's descendants had known the outcome of what God was doing in the desert at the foot of Mount Sinai, they would have responded differently. Abraham had something different in his heart, something his descendants lacked.

God once asked me to give up something I thought He had given me. It meant more to me than anything else. I had desired it for years. It was to work for a particularly well-known evangelist, one I dearly loved.

My wife and I had been offered positions on staff as assistants to this man and his wife. Not only did I love this man, but I also saw it as God's opportunity to bring to pass the dream He had implanted deep within me—that I might preach the gospel to the nations of the world.

I fully expected God to say *yes* to this wonderful offer, but He made it clear that I was to turn it down. I wept for days after refusing this offer. I knew I had obeyed God, yet I did not understand *why* He had asked such a hard thing of me. After weeks of bewilderment, I finally cried out, "God, why did You make me put this on the altar?"

He quickly answered my cry: "To see if you were serving Me or the dream."

Only then did I understand that I had been tested. In the midst of it, I had not realized what He was doing. The only things that kept me from going my own way was my love for God and my fear of Him.

ABRAHAM'S FEAR OF GOD WAS CONFIRMED

I LOVE Abraham's response to God's most difficult command. "So Abraham rose early in the morning" (Gen. 22:3). He did not talk it over with Sarah. There was no hesitation. He had decided to obey God. There were just two things that meant more to Abraham than his promised Isaac—his love and fear of God. He loved and feared God above all else.

God told Abraham to take a three-day journey. This allowed him time to ponder what he had been told to do. If there had been any wavering within him, this time period would have exposed it. When he and Isaac arrived at the designated place of worship, Abraham built an altar, bound his son, laid him on the altar, and reached for his knife. He raised the knife above Isaac's throat.

At this point, God spoke through an angel, stopping him in the midst of his obedient act. "Do not lay your hand on the lad, or do anything to him; for now I know that you fear God, since you have not withheld your son, your only son, from Me" (Gen. 22:12).

Abraham proved his fear by esteeming God's desires as even more important than his own. God knew that if Abraham passed this test, he would pass them all.

> Then Abraham lifted his eyes and looked, and there behind him was a ram caught in a thicket by its horns. So Abraham went and took the ram, and offered it up for a burnt offering instead of his son. And Abraham called the name of the place, The-Lord-Will-Provide.
> —GENESIS 22:13–14

With the completion of this test, God revealed a new facet of Himself to Abraham. He revealed Himself as Jehovah-Jireh. This revelation of God's character means "Jehovah Sees." No one since Adam had known Him in this manner. God revealed His heart to this humble man who had become His friend. The Lord was revealing to Abraham the things that to other men were yet "secrets" of His heart and character.

But it is important to understand that God did not reveal Himself as "Jehovah Sees" until Abraham had passed His test of holy fear. Many claim to know the different characteristics and attributes of God's nature, yet they have never obeyed Him in the hard places. They can sing, "Jehovah-Jireh, my provider, His grace is sufficient for me. . . . " But it is only a song until He is revealed through obedience as such. Until we pass God's test of obedience, such statements proceed from our heads and not our hearts. It is when we venture into the hard, arid wilderness of obedience that God reveals Himself as Jehovah-Jireh and friend. (See Isaiah 35:1–2.)

> Was not Abraham our father justified by works when he offered Isaac his son on the altar? Do you see that faith was working together with his works, and by works faith was made perfect? And the Scripture was fulfilled which says, "Abraham believed God, and it was accounted to him for righteousness." And he was called the friend of God.
> —JAMES 2:21–23

Notice that Abraham was justified by his corresponding works. The proof of his holy fear and faith was his obedience. To *fear* God is to *believe* God. To *believe* God is to *obey* Him. James pointed out that Abraham's obedience, fueled by his holy fear of God, resulted in friendship with God. God makes it clear:

> Friendship with the Lord is reserved for those who fear Him. With them He shares the secrets of his covenant.
> —PSALM 25:14, NLT

It could not be any clearer! Read this verse from Psalm 25 again, and hide it within your heart. Why is there an abundance of shallow preaching from pulpits? Why do Christians lack the depth of our forefathers? It is the result of a growing disease in the church. It is a virus called "An Absence of the Fear of the Lord!"

God said He reveals His secrets to those who fear Him. With whom do you share the secrets of your heart? Acquaintances or intimate friends? With intimate friends, of course. Secrets wouldn't be safe with mere acquaintances. Well, God does the same; He shares His heart only with those who fear Him.

THE MAN WHO KNEW GOD'S WAYS

THERE IS another man whom God called His friend—Moses. He was a man who knew God's ways. Exodus 33:11 says, "So the Lord spoke to Moses face to face, as a man speaks to his friend." Moses' face was unveiled for he feared God. Therefore, he was able to talk with God on an intimate level. The result was:

> He made known His ways to Moses, His acts to the children of Israel.
>
> —PSALM 103:7

Because Israel did not fear God, they were denied intimacy with Him. His ways and the secrets of His covenant were not revealed to the Israelites. They knew Him in much the same way as I know the president of the United States. I know the president by his accomplishments, provisions, and acts. The Israelites were not privy to the *why* of God's covenant. They did not understand God's motives, intentions, and the desires of His heart.

Israel only perceived God's character as it was displayed in the natural world. They often mistook His methods for "taking" or "withholding" when they did not get precisely what they wanted. It is impossible to know God merely by observing what He does in the natural world. That would be like knowing a celebrity only from the media reports. God is Spirit, and His ways are hidden from the wisdom of this natural world (John 4:24; 1 Cor. 2:6–8). God will only reveal Himself to those who fear Him. The children of Israel did not see the wisdom or understanding behind all that He was doing. Therefore, they were constantly out of step with Him.

THE FEAR OF THE LORD IS TO KNOW GOD'S WAYS

MOSES quite often knew *why* God did the things He did. The Bible describes this insight as *understanding*. In fact, Moses often knew *what* God would do before He did it, for God would reveal it to Him in advance. The Bible calls this *wisdom*. The psalmist tells us:

> The fear of the Lord is the beginning of wisdom; a good understanding have all those who do His commandments.
>
> —PSALM 111:10

To fear God is to obey Him, even when it does not seem to be to our advantage. When we fear Him, He calls us *friend*, and reveals the *why*, or the intentions and desires of His heart. We come to know Him not by His acts but His ways. Read carefully Jesus' words to His disciples at the last supper, after Judas had departed:

> You are My friends if you do whatever I command you. No longer do I call you servants, for a servant does not know what his master is doing; but I have called you friends, for all things that I heard from My Father I have made known to you.
>
> —JOHN 15:14–15

I have heard this scripture quoted as a promise of friendship with the Lord. Yet there is a very definite condition placed on this kind of friendship. The condition is:

> If you do whatever I command you.
>
> —JOHN 15:14

In the words of the psalmist, this type of friendship with God is "reserved for those who fear Him," for those who obey His Word unconditionally.

The Lord said, "No longer do I call you servants." His disciples had proven faithful as servants for three and a half years. They stayed with Jesus when other disciples left (John 6:66). There had been a season when Jesus treated them only as servants. This was a period of testing, the same as with Abraham and Moses. A new exam had begun; now His words were prophetic. The exam would conclude with the disciples' steadfast obedience in the upper room. Divine order would be established. The upper room would reveal the contents of each human heart.

Jesus said, "For a servant does not know what his master is doing; but I have called you friends, for all things that I heard from My Father I have made known to you [My friends, who fear God]." God's friends will have this gift of insight, because He shares His plans with friends.

GOD SHARES HIS PLANS WITH HIS FRIENDS

GOD SHARES the motives and intentions of His heart with His friends. He discusses His plans with them, and even confides in them.

> "Should I hide My plan from Abraham?" the Lord asked.
> —GENESIS 18:17, NLT

The Lord spoke this to the angelic servants who were with Him in the presence of Abraham. God then turned to Abraham.

> So the Lord told Abraham, "I have heard that the people of Sodom and Gomorrah are extremely evil, and that everything they do is wicked. I am going down to see whether or not these reports are true. Then I will know."
> —GENESIS 18:20–21, NLT

The Lord then confided to Abraham that impending judgment hovered over the cities of Sodom and Gomorrah. Abraham interceded and pleaded for the lives of the righteous.

Abraham asked, "Will You destroy both innocent and

guilty alike? Suppose You find fifty innocent people there within the city—will You still destroy it, and not spare it for their sakes? Surely You wouldn't do such a thing, destroying the innocent with the guilty. Why, You wouldn't do that! Should not the judge of all the earth do what is right?"

And the Lord replied, "If I find fifty innocent people in Sodom, I will spare the entire city for their sake."

—GENESIS 18:23–25, NLT

Abraham had asked that the lives of others be spared from the hand of God's judgment. Only a friend talks that way to a king or judge who has the power to execute judgment. Coming from a servant or subject, such a petition would be disrespectful. But Abraham actually entered into a negotiation process with God. Abraham then talked God down from fifty to ten, and God went on His way to search out the ten righteous people in Sodom and Gomorrah. It became obvious that the report of wickedness was true, for not even ten righteous people could be found in either city. The Lord found only Lot, Abraham's nephew, and his family.

God showed His friend Abraham what He planned to do. He confided in Abraham because Abraham feared God. His fear had raised him to the level of God's confidant.

DEFILED BY THE WORLD

LOT MAY HAVE been considered righteous, but he was also worldly. He had no more insight of impending judgment than the residents of these wicked cities. Although he was righteous, Lot was caught unaware of what was about to occur. Lot represents fleshly, carnal Christians—those who lack the burning, holy fear of God. Their relationship with the Lord is not too different from that of star-struck fans and celebrities.

This is seen by where Lot chose to dwell (among the inhabitants of Sodom and Gomorrah), the type of wife he chose, and the children he would later father through incest—the Moabites and Ammonites. Lot had chosen what had initially looked best for him, but in the end he was proven to have chosen unwisely.

In contrast, Abraham chose a separated life. He sought a city whose builder and maker was God. Lot chose fellowship with the ungodly over a separated life. Their ungodly ways whittled away at his righteousness. Eventually that exposure to ungodliness bore fruit in Lot's life and in the lives of his descendants. Lot's standards were not dictated by God; they were dictated by the society around him. Lot became "oppressed by the filthy conduct of the wicked (for that righteous man, dwelling among them, tormented his righteous soul from day to day by seeing and hearing their lawless deeds)" (2 Pet. 2:7–8).

The day of judgment would have come upon Lot as a thief in the night had it not been for God's mercy and His friendship with Abraham. God sent angelic messengers, just as He will send prophetic messengers with warning to the carnal believers in the church who remain oblivious to impending judgment.

In the urgency and fury of impending judgment, Lot's wife chose to look back. She had been warned not to look back as the Lord sent destruction upon the cities that were so full of evil. But Lot's wife had been so influenced by the world that its pull was stronger on her than the fear of the Lord. This is why Jesus warns the New Testament believers to "remember Lot's wife" (Luke 17:32).

Abraham feared God. He was God's friend. Lot lacked all but a small measure of this. He had just enough fear of the Lord to flee immediate judgment, but judgment overtook those who followed him.

Lot later proved to know neither God's heart nor His ways. James bluntly addresses believers with:

> Adulterers and adulteresses! Do you not know that friendship with the world is enmity with God? Whoever therefore wants to be a friend of the world makes himself an enemy of God.
>
> —JAMES 4:4

You cannot love the world and be a friend of God as well. James describes the condition of a believer who still seeks a relationship with the world as an adulterer, and an enemy of God. Solomon tells us:

> He who loves purity of heart and has grace on his lips, the king will be his friend.
>
> —PROVERBS 22:11

Only the pure in heart are friends with God. We must ask ourselves, *What purifies my heart? My love for God?* The love for God awakens the desire to purify, but it alone does not purify the heart. We can say we love God with great affection, yet we may still love the world. This is the entrapment of millions in the church. What force keeps us pure before this awesome King? Paul answered in clear and concise terms:

> Therefore, having these promises, beloved, let us cleanse ourselves from all filthiness of the flesh and spirit, perfecting holiness in the fear of God.
>
> —2 CORINTHIANS 7:1

True holiness or purity of heart is perfected or made mature in the fear of God! "By the fear of the Lord one departs form evil" (Prov. 16:6).

But look again at the beginning of this verse: "Therefore, having these promises . . . " What promises? They are found in the previous verses. Let's read them:

> For you are the temple of the living God. As God has said: "I will dwell in them and walk among them. I will be their God, and they shall be My people." Therefore "Come out from among them and be separate, says the Lord. Do not touch what is unclean, and I will receive you. I will be a Father to you, and you shall be My sons and daughters, says the Lord Almighty."
>
> —2 CORINTHIANS 6:16–18

This is exactly how God described His desire to dwell with the children of Israel in His glory in the wilderness. He said, "I am the Lord their God, who brought them up out of the land of Egypt, that I may dwell among them" (Exod. 29:46). And again, "I will walk among you and be your God, and you shall be My people" (Lev. 26:12). There is a parallel: He is the same holy God. He will not dwell in a defiled or unholy temple.

Let's understand the full meaning of these truths for today. God outlines the conditions or requirements of our covenant with Him that we might dwell in the presence of His glory. We must come out from among the world's system and be separate. This is a cooperative work of the fear of God and His grace. That is why Paul begins this chapter by pleading with the Corinthian church "not to receive the grace of God in vain" (2 Cor. 6:1).

In another letter Paul further clarifies his point, strongly exhorting us to pursue holiness, for if we do not, we will not see God.

> Pursue . . . holiness, without which no one will see the Lord: looking diligently lest anyone fall short of the grace of God.
>
> —HEBREWS 12:14–15

Notice again that Paul talks about receiving the grace of God in vain! We can fall short of it! He goes on to describe what keeps grace active and productive in our lives: "Let us have grace, by which we may serve God acceptably with reverence and godly fear" (v. 28). The fear of God prevents us from receiving His grace in vain. It keeps us from the desire to have a relationship with the world. It is the grace of God, coupled with the fear of God, that produces holiness or purity of heart. God promises that if we cleanse ourselves from the filth of the world, He would dwell in us in His glory. Hallelujah!

HOLY FEAR GIVES GOD
THE PLACE OF GLORY, HONOR,
REVERENCE, THANKSGIVING,
PRAISE, AND PREEMINENCE
HE DESERVES.

Fourteen

THE BLESSINGS
OF HOLY FEAR

Let us hear the conclusion of the whole matter: fear God and keep
His commandments, for this is man's all.

—ECCLESIASTES 12:13

W E HAVE extensively discussed the fear of the Lord. However, it would be impossible for us to be too thorough. The fear of the Lord is a subject that cannot be fully disclosed, no matter how many books were written. It is a continuous revelation. The same is true with God's love. Proverbs 23:17 says, "Be zealous [passionate] for the fear of the Lord all the day." We cannot become too passionate with its fire.

Because it is impossible to fully detail the fear of the Lord in finite terms, it is likewise difficult to define. It encompasses a broad spectrum like the force of the love of God. The definition I offer will be partial and merely a beginning, for it is impossible to describe in words the inner transformation of the heart. We will grow in the revealed knowledge of God throughout eternity. Proportionately, the revelation of His love and our holy fear of Him will expand.

The fear of man opposes the fear of God. The fear of man ensnares (Prov. 29:25).

We have discussed this "unholy fear" in small measure as it relates to the understanding of the fear of God. Often we understand what something is by first learning what it is not. In this light, I will define the fear of man.

To fear man is to stand in alarm, anxiety, awe, dread, suspicion, or cowering before mortal men. Those entrapped by this type of fear will live on the run, hiding from harm or reproach, constantly avoiding rejection and confrontation. They become so busy safeguarding themselves that they are soon ineffective in their service for God. Afraid of what man can do, they deny God what He deserves.

The fear of God includes, but is not limited to, respecting and reverencing Him, for we are told to tremble at His presence. Holy fear gives God the place of glory, honor, reverence, thanksgiving, praise, and preeminence He deserves. (Notice it is what He deserves, not what we think He deserves.)

God holds this preeminent position in our hearts and lives as we esteem His desires over and above our own, hating what He hates and loving what He loves, trembling in His presence and at His Word.

Hear this and meditate on it:

You will serve whom you fear.

If you fear God, you will serve Him. If you fear man, you will serve man. You must choose.

Now you can understand why Solomon, after an entire life of both success and hardship, could say:

> Let us hear the conclusion of the whole matter: fear God
> and keep His commandments, for this is man's all.
> —ECCLESIASTES 12:13

Solomon pursued wisdom throughout his entire life. He obtained it, and it ushered in great success. However, he went through a period of torment and vexation in his latter years. The fear of God in his heart had waned. He no longer obeyed the commandments of God. He married foreign wives and served their gods.

At the close of his life, he looked back and after much meditation wrote the Book of Ecclesiastes. In this book, Solomon examines life apart from the fear of God. His response to every probing question was, "Vanity!"

At the very end of the book, he concludes that the whole matter of life is summed up in fearing God and keeping His commandments!

THE BLESSINGS OF FEARING GOD

I ENCOURAGE YOU to read through your Bible, and with the use of a concordance locate each scripture that relates to the fear of God. Record them for future reference. In my search, I compiled over fifty typewritten pages. I found some very definite promises for those who fear the Lord. Allow me to share just a few.

THE FEAR OF GOD . . .

- *positions our hearts to receive answers*

Who, in the days of His flesh, when He had offered up prayers and supplications, with vehement cries and tears to Him who was able to save Him from death, and was heard because of His godly *fear.*

—HEBREWS 5:7

- *assures that God's great goodness abounds*

Oh, how great is Your goodness, which You have laid up for those who *fear* You, which You have prepared for those who trust in You in the presence of the sons of men!

—PSALM 31:19

- *promises angelic protection*

The angel of the Lord encamps all around those who *fear* Him, and delivers them.

—PSALM 34:7

- *secures God's continual attention*

Behold, the eye of the Lord is on those who *fear* Him, on those who hope in His mercy.

—PSALM 33:18

- *supplies His provision*

Oh, *fear* the Lord, you His saints! There is no want to those who *fear* Him.

—PSALM 34:9

- *contains great mercy*

For as the heavens are high above the earth, so great is His mercy toward those who *fear* Him.

—PSALM 103:11

- *provides assurance of food*

He has given food to those who *fear* Him; He will ever be mindful of His covenant.

—PSALM 111:5

- *promises protection*

You who *fear* the Lord, trust in the Lord; He is their help and their shield.

—PSALM 115:11

- *fulfills our desires and delivers us from harm*

He will fulfill the desire of those who *fear* Him; He also will hear their cry and save them.

—Psalm 145:19

- *provides wisdom, understanding, and time management*

The *fear* of the Lord is the beginning of wisdom, and the knowledge of the Holy One is understanding. For by me your days will be multiplied, and years of life will be added to you.

—Proverbs 9:10–11

- *is our confidence and protection in the face of death*

In the *fear* of the Lord there is strong confidence, and His children will have a place of refuge. The *fear* of the Lord is a fountain of life, to turn one away from the snares of death.

—Proverbs 14:26–27

- *provides peace of mind*

Better is a little with the *fear* of the Lord, than great treasure with trouble.

—Proverbs 15:16

- *results in complete satisfaction*

The *fear* of the Lord leads to life, and he who has it will abide in satisfaction; he will not be visited with evil.

—Proverbs 19:23

- *leads to riches, honor, and life*

By humility and the *fear* of the Lord are riches and honor and life.

—Proverbs 22:4

- *will keep us on the path*

And I will make an everlasting covenant with them, that I will not turn away from doing them good; but I will put My *fear* in their hearts so that they will not depart from Me.

—Jeremiah 32:40

- *produces a secure household*

And so it was, because the midwives *feared* God, that He provided households for them.

—Exodus 1:21

- *provides clarity and direction*

Who is the man that *fears* the Lord? Him shall He teach in the way He chooses.

—Psalm 25:12

- *results in enjoyment of our labor, and full, rewarding lives*

How happy are those who *fear* the Lord—all who follow His ways! You will enjoy the fruit of your labor. How happy you will be! How rich your life! Your wife will be like a fruitful vine, flourishing within your home. And look at all those children! There they sit around your table as vigorous and healthy as young olive trees. That is the Lord's reward for those who *fear* Him.

—Psalm 128:1–4, NLT

- *produces successful leadership*

Moreover you shall select from all the people able men, such as *fear* God, men of truth, hating covetousness; and place such over them to be rulers of thousands, rulers of hundreds, rulers of fifties, and rulers of tens.

—Exodus 18:21

The God of Israel said, the Rock of Israel spoke to me: "He who rules over men must be just, ruling in the *fear* of God."
—2 SAMUEL 23:3

These are but a few of God's promises for those who fear Him. There are many more. I encourage you to find them in your time of reading and studying God's Word.

Epilogue

THE FEAR of God should burn bright in our hearts no matter how long we've been saved. In fact, it is a key element to receiving salvation.

Paul proclaims, "Those among you who fear God, to you the word of this salvation has been sent" (Acts 13:26).

Without this holy fear, we will not recognize our need for salvation.

No matter where you are spiritually, I encourage you to pray with me. If you have not previously submitted yourself to the lordship of Jesus, now is the time to turn your life over to Him. You have heard the Word, and faith has risen in your heart. If the Holy Spirit has brought deep conviction and you are ready to turn from the world and sin and give yourself wholly to Him, now is the time. It's time to make the decision to completely submit your life to His lordship. It's time to confirm it through prayer.

Father in Heaven, in the name of Jesus, I humble myself and come to You to seek Your mercy and grace. I have heard Your Word, and the desire to love, fear, and know You now burns in my heart. I ask forgiveness for the life I have lived irreverently before coming to You. I repent of all disrespect and hypocrisy I have tolerated in my life.

I turn to You, Jesus, as my Savior and Lord. You are my Master, and I give my life completely to You. Fill me with Your love and holy fear. I desire to know You intimately in a deeper dimension than I have ever known anyone or anything else. I acknowledge my need and dependency for and on Your Holy Spirit and ask that You would fill me now.

Lord, Your Word promises that as I turn to You with all my heart the Holy Spirit will reveal Your true image and character to me, and I will be changed from glory to glory. Like Moses, I ask to see Your face. In this secret place, I will be changed.

Lord Jesus, thank You for the abundant mercy and grace You've extended to me. For all You have already done and all You are about to do, I give You the glory, honor, and praise, both now and forever. Amen.

Now to Him who is able to keep you from stumbling, and to present you faultless before the presence of His glory with exceeding joy, to God our Savior, who alone is wise, be glory and majesty, dominion and power, both now and forever. Amen.

—JUDE 24–25

Other Books By John and Lisa Bevere:

VICTORY IN THE WILDERNESS by John Bevere
God, Where Are You?

Is this the cry of your heart? Does it seem your spiritual progress in the Lord has come to a halt—or even regressed? You wonder if you have missed God or somehow displeased Him, but that is not the case . . . you've just arrived at the wilderness! Now, don't misunderstand the purpose of the wilderness. It is not God's rejection, but the season of His preparation in your life. God intends for you to have *Victory in the Wilderness.*

Understanding this season is crucial to the successful completion of your journey. It is the road traveled by patriarchs and prophets in preparation for a fresh move of God.

Some issues addressed in this book:
- How God refines
- Is the wilderness necessary?
- Pressing through dry times
- What is the focus of the true prophetic?
- Why *where you are* is vital to *where you're going*

THE VOICE OF ONE CRYING by John Bevere
A Prophetic Message for Today!

God is restoring the prophetic to turn the hearts of His people to Him. Yet often this office is reduced to merely one who predicts the future by a word of knowledge or wisdom . . . rather than a declaration of the church's true condition and destiny. Many, fed up with hype and superficial ministry, are ready to receive the true prophetic message.

Some issues addressed in this book:
- Genuine vs. counterfeit conversion
- Message of the true prophetic
- Recognizing false prophets
- The Elijah anointing
- Idolatry in America
- Exposing deception

BREAKING INTIMIDATION by John Bevere
How to Overcome Fear and Release the Gift of God in Your Life

Countless Christians battle intimidation. Yet they wrestle with the side effects rather than the source. Intimidation is rooted in the fear of man. Proverbs 29:25 says, "The fear of man brings a snare . . ." This snare limits us so we don't reach our full potential.

Paul admonished Timothy, "The gift of God in you is dormant because you're intimidated!" (2 Tim. 1:6–7, paraphrased). An intimidated believer loses his position of spiritual authority. Without this authority his gifting from God remains dormant.

The Bible is filled with examples of God's people facing intimidation. Some overcame while others were overcome. This book is an in-depth look at these ancient references and present-day scenarios. The goal: to expose intimidation, break its fearful grip, and release God's gift and dominion in your life.

This is an urgent message for every child of God who desires to reach their full potential in their walk with Christ. Don't allow fear to hold you back!

OUT OF CONTROL AND LOVING IT! by Lisa Bevere

Is your life a whirlwind of turmoil? Are you hating it? It is because you are in control! In this candid and honest book, Lisa challenges you to relinquish control of your life to God. Are you tired of pretending to be free only to remain captive? This book contains in-depth insight into how fear causes us to hold on when we should let go! Are you holding on? Abandon yourself to God's care!

- Escaping captivity
- Overcoming anger
- Your past is not your future
- Conquering fear
- The strongholds of gossip
- Self neglect vs. self denial

"This is one of the most powerful books I have read on the subject on control."
—*Marilyn Hickey, Marilyn Hickey Ministries*

"Next to the Bible, this book is perhaps the nost important book a woman will ever read . . ." —*Lindsay Roberts, Oral Roberts Ministries*

<u>Endorsed by additional women leaders:</u>
Sharon Daugherty, Suzanne Hinn, Dr. Fuschia Pickett, Mary Brown, Gina Pearson, Cheryl Salem, and Paula White.

THE BAIT OF SATAN *by John Bevere*
Your Response Determines Your Future

This book exposes one of the most deceptive snares Satan uses to get believers out of the will of God. It is the trap of offense.

Most who are ensnared do not even realize it. But everyone must be made aware of this trap, because Jesus said, "It is impossible that offenses will not come" (Luke 17:1).

The question is not, "Will you encounter the bait of Satan?" Rather it is, "How will you respond?" *Your response determines your future!* Don't let another person's sin or mistake affect your relationship with God!

> "This book by my friend John Bevere is strong, strong, strong! I found new help from his fresh insights and uncompromising desire to help each of us recognize Satan's baits and avoid them at all costs."
> —*Oral Roberts, Oral Roberts University*

THE DEVIL'S DOOR *by John Bevere*

In *The Bait of Satan,* John Bevere exposed the devil's number-one trap for believers today. In *The Devil's Door,* he reveals the easiest way the enemy gains access in the lives of Christians—through rebellion. Satan cleverly deceives believers into thinking that submission is bondage and that rebellion is freedom. This revealing book exposes the devil's deception, blocks his entrance into your life, and helps you enjoy God's blessing and protection.

■ This book contains challenging and life-changing truths.
■ What is the source of true kingdom authority?
■ Learn to shut this door and lock it!

Audio/Visual Messages:

By John and Lisa Bevere

Videos
"The Bait of Satan"
"The Baptism of Fire"
"Breaking Intimidation"
"Does God Know You?"
"Don't Faint Before Your Harvest"
"The Fear of the Lord"
"Passion for His Presence"
"You Asked For It"

Audiocassette Series (3 tapes)
"Armed to Suffer"
"By Order of the King"
"The Fear of the Lord"
"Pursue the High Call"
"Standing Strong in a World of Compromise"
"The Training Ground of Champions"
"Walking With God"
"Out of Control and Loving It!" (Lisa Bevere)

To order call 1-800-648-1477 (U.S. only)
or 407-889-9617

PLEASE CONTACT JOHN BEVERE MINISTRIES:
■ To receive JBM's free newsletter, *The Messenger*
■ To receive a free and complete color catalog
■ To inquire about inviting the ministry of
John and Lisa Bevere to your organization

JOHN BEVERE MINISTRIES
P. O Box 2002, Apopka, FL 32704-2002 U.S.A.
Tel: 407-889-9617; Fax: 407-889-2065